What others have said about
Amo, Amas, Amat and More:

"A book for all word buffs."   —John Ciardi

"Scholarly yet humorous renderings of Latin expressions."
—Don Oldenburg, *Washington Post*

"Since I could go on to the point of tedium in praising this book
and the pleasure I took from it, let me stress its suitability for
any literate person who may not want to astonish anyone but
merely wants to be well-informed....it's a delightful book."
—Herbert A. Kenny, *National Review*

"Thoroughly refreshing...entertaining for its smart talk, for its
lively historical notes on everyone from Julius Caesar to Cesare
Borgia, and for its inclusion of favorite one-liners from a host
of Roman writers, especially Horace, Virgil, Juvenal, and
Martial....It proves that Latin persists and shows why."
—*The Classical Outlook*

"A handy compilation of idioms selected from classical writings
and legal and ecclesiastical terminology...an entertaining book
for browsers."   —*Library Journal*

Amo, Amas, Amat and More

How to Use Latin to Your Own Advantage and to the Astonishment of Others

EUGENE EHRLICH

Introduction by
WILLIAM F. BUCKLEY, JR.

A Hudson Group Book

Harper & Row, Publishers, New York
Grand Rapids, Philadelphia, St. Louis, San Francisco
London, Singapore, Sydney, Tokyo, Toronto

A hardcover edition of this book is published by Harper & Row, Publishers, Inc.

AMO, AMAS, AMAT AND MORE. Copyright © 1985 by Eugene Ehrlich. Introduction copyright © 1985 by William F. Buckley, Jr. All rights reserved. Printed in the United States of America. No part of this book may be used or reproduced in any manner whatsoever without written permission except in the case of brief quotations embodied in critical articles and reviews. For information address Harper & Row, Publishers, Inc., 10 East 53rd Street, New York, N.Y. 10022. Published simultaneously in Canada by Fitzhenry & Whiteside Limited, Toronto.

First PERENNIAL LIBRARY edition published 1987

Designer: C. Linda Dingler

Library of Congress Cataloging-in-Publication Data

Ehrlich, Eugene H.
  Amo, amas, amat and more.

  "Perennial Library."
  Includes indexes.
  1. Latin language.   I. Title.
PA2057.E38 1987   470   84-48594
ISBN 0-06-272017-1 (pbk.)

00 01 **RRD - H** 20 19 18 17 16

To Norma

Contents

Acknowledgments

I wish particularly to thank Christopher Dadian, of the Department of Classics, The Johns Hopkins University, who gave thoughtful attention to the pronunciation scheme employed in this book as well as to the translations provided. If any errors are still to be found in the work, they are my own responsibility. All that can be said at this time is *errare humanum est*, and while I would appreciate hearing from readers who find these errors, I would also hope to be forgiven.

My associates at The Hudson Group gave me support all through the joy of compiling this book. My longtime collaborator Gorton Carruth put up with my divided attention to other responsibilities. Hayden Carruth taught me the rudiments of the IBM Personal Computer so that an ancient language could be treated, perhaps for the first time ever, within the confines of a cathode ray tube. Only once did his ministrations fail to rescue me from the effects of my computer illiteracy: At one time I lost an entire section of the book somewhere within the computer memory, and for all I know, it is lurking there to this day. Raymond Hand, Jr., helped free me for work on this book and assisted with the free renderings of certain Latin proverbs.

Carol Cohen, Harper & Row's Editorial Director of Trade Reference Books, showed enthusiasm for this book right from the start and supported me with encouragement and guidance all the way to completion. Her ideas for developing the project helped immeasurably.

The above-mentioned personal computer obviates acknowledgment of a typist's help, but a final word must be added for the help in indexing supplied by Felice Levy, who has participated with me on many editorial projects.

Preface

The idea for this book came quickly, as do most of my ideas for books. The execution was not as fast. Years of collecting expressions suitable for inclusion, followed by months of translation and writing, have finally yielded a volume I hope will prove entertaining as well as instructive for readers.

A word must be said about the choice of expressions. Utility was the principal criterion. There is no doubt that readers are plagued by writers and speakers who blithely drop Latin phrases into their English sentences with no hint of translation. Without questioning the motives of the Latin-droppers, one can safely say that most modern audiences require some assistance. Word-for-word translations provided in some English dictionaries do not always suffice, so the attempt is made in many entries of this book to supply more enlightening free translations as well as literal translations. Besides helping readers and listeners to cope with Latin used by others, it is hoped that *Amo, Amas, Amat* . . . will spare its readers the ignominy of an infelicitous choice when they venture into Latin. The most common misuse I encounter is the confusion of *e.g.* with *i.e.*, but there are many others. Once *e.g.* and *i.e.* were accepted for inclusion in this book, it became necessary to treat in the list of entries all but the most arcane scholarly abbreviations and expressions.

Medical and pharmacological Latin were never serious candidates for inclusion: Prescriptions are filled a million or more times a day without the Latin once required to say "take twice a day" and the like. But Latin still is seen in everyday writing about matters of law, and the law is a serious matter. The problem was to limit the number of entries of this type to those most frequently encountered—consider *in re* and *corpus delicti* and a multitude of others. Fortunately, engineers, computer scientists, electronics experts, and other modern wizards hit their stride long after Latin had disappeared from most school curricula, so they make no contribution to this volume despite the fact that modern Latin words are continually being devised to enable the Vatican to deal knowledgeably with modern science and technology, just as modern Hebrew must face this requirement. Of course, it is not only ancient languages that must cope with this problem. Modern English, in fact, brings new words into use every day, sometimes inventing them—often from Latin and Greek sources—and sometimes adding meanings to existing English words. Indeed, where appropriate, English accomplishes its purpose by borrowing existing words from modern foreign languages.

While the majority of the entries in this book date back to classical times, there is some treatment of phrases that came into use during the Middle Ages. As will be seen, some of the Latin included in the entry list is used—should one say was used?—in church services.

Once the list of candidate entries had grown to reflect these many sources and areas of learning, a much more difficult task had to be accomplished, that of selecting, among a vast number of available maxims and proverbs, those that would be most interesting and useful for the modern reader. One principle of selection was the inherent wisdom reflected in the thought. Another was the insight into a civilization implicit in a thought. As I worked through the entry list again and again, I was struck by the universality of people's problems throughout the ages, and the satisfying solutions afforded, despite the often contradictory nature of these solutions. It is hoped that the reader will share the pleasure of this recognition.

So *Amo, Amas, Amat* . . . took form, sometimes growing recklessly and demanding to be pruned, at other times crying out for fuller treatment of a particular topic.

Now a word must be said about the pronunciations supplied in this book. No one knows just how Latin was pronounced by the Romans. I was taught by my instructors at Townsend Harris High School and the City College of New York to pronounce the name *Caesar* as though the first letter were a *k*. Others may pronounce that first letter as though it were *ch*, as in *chew*. This dispute, along with several other questions of pronunciation, is moot. Let me assure the reader, however, that using the pronunciations offered in this book will make it possible to pronounce Latin without incurring the scorn of most people who have studied the language in American public schools.

EUGENE EHRLICH

Pronunciation Notes

This volume uses a respelling scheme to represent the sounds of Latin. Stresses are indicated by typographic means.

Stress. Stressed syllables are shown in capital letters, and unstressed syllables as well as words of a single syllable are shown in lower case. Thus, *Deo* (to God) is pronounced DAY-oh, *familia* (family) is pronounced fah-MIH-lee-ah, and *ars* (art) is pronounced ahrs.

Vowels. Like English vowels, certain Latin vowels have various qualities. The samples given here help in sounding out the Latin words in the pages that follow.

Pronunciation		English	Latin Word	Latin Pronunciation
AH *or* ah	*as in*	far	*fabula*	FAH-buu-lah
AY *or* ay	*as in*	fake	*fecere*	FAY-keh-reh
AW *or* aw	*as in*	tall	*hominem*	HAW-mih-nem
E *or* e	*as in*	pet	*et*	et
EH *or* eh	*as in*	pet	*petere*	PEH-teh-reh
EE *or* ee	*as in*	sweet	*vita*	WEE-tah
IH *or* ih	*as in*	dig	*signum*	SIH-gnuum
OH *or* oh	*as in*	both	*dolor*	DOH-lawr
OO *or* oo	*as in*	moon	*unum*	OO-nuum
UU *or* uu	*as in*	put	*unum*	OO-nuum

After the letter *q*, and sometimes after *g* and *s*, the Latin *u* has the sound made by the English *w*. This is no surprise for speakers of English. Consider the words *quick*, *guava*, and *suave*. Thus, *quandoque* (sometimes) is pronounced kwahn-DOH-kweh.

Diphthongs. Like English, in which, for example, the diphthong *oi* is given a single sound (as in *point*) and *ou* is given a single sound (as in *loud*), Latin has its share of diphthongs.

Diphthong	Pronunciation	English		Latin Word	Latin Pronunciation
ae	Ī	*as in*	my	*Caesar*	KĪ-sahr
ae	ĭ	*as in*	my	*lacrimae*	LAH-krih-mī
au	OW or ow	*as in*	now	*Augustus*	ow-GUU-stuus
ei	AY or ay	*as in*	faint	*deinde*	DAYN-deh
eu	HEHOO	*(no equivalent)*		*eheu*	eh-HEHOO*
oe	OY or oy	*as in*	boy	*proelium*	PROY-lee-uum
ui	OOEE or ooee	*as in*	phooey	*huius*	HOOEE-uus

*Pronounce as a single sound: HEHOO as a blend of HEH and OO, not pronouncing the second H.

Consonants. Latin consonants are pronounced in the same way as their English equivalents, with the following exceptions.

1. The Latin *c* is pronounced as though it were a *k*. Thus, *Cicero* is pronounced KIH-keh-roh.

2. The Latin *g* is always pronounced like the *g* in the English word *give*. Thus, *geometria* (geometry) is pronounced gay-oh-MEH-tree-ah, and *dignus* (worthy) is pronounced DIH-gnuus.

3. The Latin *s* is always pronounced like the *s* in the English word *set* or *pest* or *pets*. Thus, *semper paratus* (always ready) is pronounced SEM-pehr pah-RAH-tuus.

4. A *j* is often seen before a vowel in some Latin texts where one would expect to see an *i*. Whichever letter is used, the sound is taken as an initial *y*, as in the English word *young*. This means that the *i* (as well as the *j*) functions as a consonant. Thus, the Latin word for *law*, whether spelled *ius* or *jus*, is pronounced yoos, but when *i* appears before

a consonant, *i* is pronounced as a vowel. As speakers of a modern language, we are not dismayed by such apparent anomalies. Consider the pronunciation of the English word *union* (initial syllable YOON) and that of the English word *unable* (initial syllable un).

5. The Latin *v* is always pronounced as though it were a *w*. Thus, *veni, vidi, vici* is pronounced WAY-nee, WEE-dee, WEE-kee; and *ave atque vale* is pronounced AH-weh AHT-kweh WAH-lay.

English pronunciation. In many entries in this volume, Latin phrases are given English pronunciations as well as Latin pronunciations. This is done for Latin phrases that have been taken into the English language and given distinctive pronunciations. Such words are respelled for the reader in readily recognizable letter combinations to show the English pronunciations.

In the case of one sound, respelling is not sufficient, so an additional symbol is needed to approximate English pronunciation. The symbol ə is used to indicate the indistinct vowel sound represented by the first syllable of the English word *ago* (ə-GOH) and the second syllable of the English word *ever* (EV-ər). Thus, while the Latin pronunciation of *sui generis* is given as SOO-ee GEH-neh-rihs, the English pronunciation appears as SOO-ee JEN-ə-rəs.

amo   I love
amas you love
amat he, she, or it loves

. . .

—the beginning of the paradigm of
a first conjugation Latin verb
in the present indicative

Amo, Amas, Amat and More

Introduction

by *William F. Buckley, Jr.*

It is not plain to me why I was asked to write the introduction to this book. (There are true Latinists around. Not in abundance, but for instance one thinks of Garry Wills, or Ernest Van den Haag, just to mention two noisy, and brilliant, writers.) Nor is it obvious why I accepted the invitation (the little stipend is being forwarded to charity).

I suppose I am asked because the few Latin phrases I am comfortable with I tend to use without apology. For instance, for some reason I find it handier even in idiomatic exchanges to say "per impossibile" over against, say, "assuming that the impossible were actually to take place." Nor is the usefulness of *per impossibile* sui generis—if you see the kind of situation one is capable of falling into. And, of course, there are those Latin phrases that have a utilitarian function, as for instance the lawyers' "nolle prosequi," which has become so thoroughly transliterated as to have acquired English conjugational life: thus, "The case against Dr. Arbuthnot was nol-prossed"—the lawyer's vernacular for "The prosecutor decided not to prosecute the case against Dr. Arbuthnot."

So, there are those Latin phrases—and, really, there are not so many of them—that cling to life because they seem to perform useful duties without any challenger rising up to take their place in English. Sometimes these special exemptions from vernacularization in the mother tongue derive from the distinctive inflection that flows in from the Latin. There is no English substitute, really, for "He faced the problem *ad hoc*," which is much easier than the cumbersome alternative in English ("He faced the problem with exclusive concern given to the circumstances that particularly surrounded it"). Other Latin phrases, the kind against which Fowler inveighed, have the sense of being dragged in, and the reader, when he comes across them, will judge on the basis of circumstances whether he is on to a felicitous intonation communicated by the Latin and not by the English. The scholarly Mr. Ehrlich, for instance, includes in this collection "Ab asino lanam," giving as the English meaning (which is different from the English translation), "blood from a stone." And further elucidating, "Anyone who tries to achieve the impossible is doomed to failure. Thus, an attempt to get *ab asino lanam*, literally, 'wool from an ass,' will inevitably fail." The above is for the scholar, not the practitioner of idiom.

But then why not? Mr. Ehrlich, in his introduction, touches on the difficulty of assembling a list meagerly. Inevitably some readers would be dissatisfied. For all one knows, there is someone about who day in and day out denounces efforts to reason with the Soviets as ventures *ab asino lanam*, and it would ruin their life if a collection of Latin sayings were published that left out that expression. Better, then, to include "ab asino lanam," and the kitchen sink; which Mr. Ehrlich does, and I am very glad that he decided to do so.

Probably the principal Latin-killer this side of the Huns was Vatican II. The other day, sitting alongside a Jesuit college president, I mentioned, by way of indicating the distinctive training of English Jesuits, that my schoolmasters at Beaumont College, when engaged in faculty discussions, addressed each other in Latin. He replied matter-of-factly that so it had been with him and his classmates. "But now, after fifteen years, I would have a problem with relatively simple Latin."

No doubt about it, the generations of Catholic priests trained in Latin, and the seepage of Latin to parishioners, students, altar boys, will diminish, drying up the spring which for so many centuries watered the general knowledge of Latin, and held out almost exclusively, after the virtual desertion of Latin from curricula in which it held, in e.g. English public schools, an absolutely patriarchal position. But it is not likely that the remaining bits and pieces will all be extirpated by the vernacular juggernaut. And even if that were so, it would happen generations down the line. Meanwhile I know of no book to contend in usefulness with that of Mr. Ehrlich, who has given us this resourceful, voluminous, and appetizing smorgasbord.

Dramatis Personae

Caesar. *Gaius Iulius Caesar*. 100–44 B.C. Born at Rome. Soldier, statesman. *Bellum Gallicum* (*The Gallic War*), *Bellum civile* (*The Civil War*).

Cato. *Marcus Porcius Cato*. 234–149 B.C. Born in Tusculum, in central Italy. Roman statesman. *De agricultura* (*On Agriculture*).

Catullus. *Gaius Valerius Catullus*. 84?–54? B.C. Born at Verona, in Cisalpine Gaul. Best known for his tempestuous love affair with a Roman gentlewoman (probably the notorious Clodia), whom he immortalized in his poems under the pseudonym Lesbia. *Carmina* (*Poems*).

Cicero. *Marcus Tullius Cicero*. 106–43 B.C. Born at Arpinum in central Italy. Jurist, statesman, writer, philosopher. *Orationes* (*Orations*), *Rhetorica* (*Writings on Rhetoric*), *Philosophica* (*Political and Philosophical Writings*), *Epistulae* (*Letters*).

Claudian. *Claudius Claudianus*. A.D. 4th cent.–c. 404. From Alexandria. A speaker of Greek. Came to Italy and mastered Latin, which was the language of his writings. Court poet under the emperor Honorius; his poetry eulogized his patrons. *De consulatu Honorii* (*On the Consulship of Honorius*), *De consulatu Stilichonis* (*On the Consulship of Stilicho*).

Epicurus.   341–270 B.C. Born at Samos, a Greek island in the Aegean. Moral and natural philosopher. Our knowledge of his system derives to a great extent from the Roman poet Lucretius. *Epistulae* (*Letters*), Κύριαι Δοξαι (*Kyriai Doxai*, *Principal Doctrines*).

Horace.   *Quintus Horatius Flaccus*. 65–8 B.C. Born at Venusia, in southern Italy. Member of the literary circle brought together by Maecenas under the patronage of the emperor Augustus. *Carmina* (*Odes*), *Epodi* (*Epodes*), *Satirae* (*Satires*), *Epistulae* (*Verse Letters*), *Ars Poetica* (*The Poetic Art*).

Juvenal.   *Decimus Iunius Iuvenalis*. A.D. 1st–2nd cent. Born at Aquinum, Italy. Author of verse satires attacking corruption of Roman society. *Satirae* (*Satires*).

Livy.   *Titus Livius*. 59 B.C.–A.D. 17 or 64 B.C.–A.D. 12. Born at Padua, in northeastern Italy. Historian. *Ab urbe condita* ([History of Rome] *from the Founding of the City*).

Lucan.   *Marcus Annaeus Lucanus*. A.D. 39–65. Born at Cordoba, in Spain. Courtier in the reign of Nero. Fell from grace and eventually was forced to commit suicide after becoming implicated in the Pisonian conspiracy. *Pharsalia*.

Lucretius.   *Titus Lucretius Carus*. Prob. 94–55 B.C. Probably member of an aristocratic Roman family, the Lucretii. Poet and philosopher. *De rerum natura* (*On the Nature of the Universe*).

Manilius.   *Marcus Manilius*. 1st cent. B.C.–A.D. 1st cent. Facts of his life unknown. *Astronomica* (a didactic poem on astrology).

Marcus Aurelius.   *Marcus Aurelius Antoninus*. A.D. 121–180. Roman emperor. *Meditationes* (*Meditations*).

Martial.   *Marcus Valerius Martialus*. c. A.D. 40–c. 104. Born at Bilbilis, in Spain. Depicted Roman society in epigrammatic verse. *Epigrammata* (*Epigrams*).

Ovid.   *Publius Ovidius Naso*. 43 B.C.–A.D. 17. Born at Sulmo, in central Italy. Intended by his father for a legal career, but gave it up to devote himself to poetry. Member of the literary circle of Messalla. Exiled to an island in the Black Sea by Augustus, who was offended by Ovid's *Ars Amatoria*, though there may have been other offenses as well. *Amores* (*Love Poems*), *Ars Amatoria* (*The Amatory Art*), *Metamorphoses*.

Persius. *Aulus Persius Flaccus*. A.D. 34–62. Born at Volaterrae, in northern Italy. Stoic satirist. *Satirae* (*Satires*).

Petronius. *Petronius Arbiter*. A.D. 1st cent. Probably the courtier referred to by Tacitus as Nero's *arbiter elegantiae*. *Satyricon*.

Phaedrus. c. 15 B.C.–c. A.D. 50. A Thracian, born a slave. Eventually became freedman in the household of the emperor Augustus. *Fabulae* (*Fables*).

Plautus. *Titus Maccius Plautus*. 3rd–2nd cent. B.C. Born at Sarsina, in central Italy. Author of comic dramas based on Greek originals.

Pliny the Elder.   *Gaius Plinius*. A.D. 23/4–79. Born at Comum, now Como, in north central Italy. Military commander in Germany, provincial administrator, counselor to emperors Vespasian and Titus. *Naturalis historia* (*Natural History*).

Pliny the Younger.   *Gaius Plinius Caecilius Secundus*. c. A.D. 66–c. 112. Nephew and adopted son of Pliny the Elder. Senatorial career; lawyer, civil administrator. *Epistulae* (*Letters*).

Plutarch. *L.* (?) *Mestrius Plutarchus*. Before A.D. 50–after 120. Born and lived most of his life in Chaeronea, in northeastern Greece. Prolific (over 200 titles attributed to him) and influential. *Moralia*, *Vitae* (*Lives*).

Publilius Syrus. 1st cent. B.C. Came to Rome as a slave, perhaps from Antioch. Author of mimes. *Sententiae* (*Maxims*).

Quintilian. *Marcus Fabius Quintilianus*. c. A.D. 30–before 100. Born at Calagurris, in Spain. Teacher of rhetoric; among his pupils was Pliny the Younger. *Institutio oratoria* (*The Teaching of Oratory*).

Seneca the Elder.   *Lucius Annaeus Seneca*. c. 55 B.C.–

between A.D. 37 and 41. Born at Cordoba, in Spain. Student of and writer on rhetoric. *Controversiae*, *Suasoriae*.

Seneca the Younger. *Lucius Annaeus Seneca*. Between 4 and 1 B.C.–A.D. 65. Born at Cordoba, in Spain. Son of Seneca the Elder, counsellor to Nero, philosopher, poet. *Dialogi* (*Dialogues*), *Naturales quaestiones* (*Natural Questions*, inquiries in physical science), *Apocolocyntosis* (*The Pumpkinification* [of the emperor Claudius]), *Tragedies*, *Epigrams*.

Suetonius. *Gaius Suetonius Tranquillus*. c. A.D. 69–? Practiced law briefly, held various posts in the imperial service, secretary to the emperor Hadrian. *De vita Caesarum* (*Lives of the Caesars* [from Julius to Domitian]).

Tacitus. *Cornelius Tacitus*. c. 56 A.D.–after 115. Probably from northern Italy or Gaul. Historian, held several official posts. *Annales* (*Annals*), *Historiae* (*Histories*), *Agricola* ([biography of his father-in-law, Cnaius Iulius] *Agricola*), *Germania*.

Terence. *Publius Terentius Afer*. c. 190–159 B.C. Born in North Africa, brought to Rome as a slave. Author of comic dramas adapted from Greek models by Apollodorus of Carystus and Menander. *Andria* (*The Girl from Andros*), *Hecyra* (*The Mother-in-Law*), *Heauton timorumenos* (*The Self-Punisher*), *Eunuchus* (*The Eunuch*), *Phormio*, *Adelphi* (*The Brothers*).

Tertullian. *Quintus Septimius Florens Tertullianus*. c. A.D. 160–c. 240. Born at Carthage, in North Africa. Trained as a lawyer. Converted to Christianity at age 35, wrote in defense of his new faith, and on moral, ethical, religious problems.

Varro. *Marcus Terentius Varro*. 116–27 B.C. Born at Reate, in central Italy. Wrote on language, education, history, biography, philosophy, music, medicine, architecture, literary history and philology. *De lingua latina* (*On the Latin Language*).

Vegetius. *Flavius Vegetius Renatus*. A.D. 4th–5th cent. Bureaucrat in the imperial service. *Epitome rei militaris* (*Manual of Military Affairs*).

Virgil. *Publius Vergilius Maro*. 70–19 B.C. Born near Man-
tua, in northeastern Italy. Early in his career deeply in-
fluenced by Catullus, member of the literary circle of
Asinius Pollio. Later, through Maecenas, came under the
patronage of the emperor Augustus. *Aeneid*, *Georgics*,
Eclogues.

ab absurdo
ahb ahb-SUUR-doh
from the absurd

One who argues *ab absurdo* seeks to establish the validity of his position by pointing out the absurdity of his opponent's position. While an argument *ab absurdo* may have the effect of demolishing one's opponent's position in debate, it usually does not of itself prove the validity of one's own position.

ab aeterno
ahb ī-TEHR-noh
since the beginning of time

Anything that has existed *ab aeterno*, literally "from eternity," has no assignable date of origin. This phrase can be used to describe almost any human folly: "Wars have been fought *ab aeterno*."

ab asino lanam
ahb AH-sih-noh LAH-nahm
blood from a stone

Anyone who tries to achieve the impossible is doomed to failure. Thus, an attempt to get *ab asino lanam*, literally "wool from an ass," will inevitably fail.

11

ab extra
ahb EHK-strah
from the outside

This phrase, the opposite of AB INTRA, finds use in such thoughts as "We are mistaken in believing that peace will come to the Middle East through the efforts *ab extra* of world powers."

ab imo pectore
ahb EE-moh PEH-ktaw-reh
from the heart

When we speak from the heart, we speak sincerely, but the Romans spoke *ab imo pectore*, literally "from the bottom of the breast (or chest)."

ab incunabulis
ahb ihn-koo-NAH-buu-lees
from infancy

The Latin word **incunabula** may be translated as "cradle, swaddling clothes, infancy, or origin." The English "incunabula" refers to the earliest stage or beginning of anything, but most often to copies of books that date back to the period before A.D. 1500, when the use of movable type in printing was in its formative stage. The Latin *ab incunabulis* has nothing to do with books.

ab initio
ahb ih-NIH-tee-oh
from the beginning

The Latin equivalent of "from the start" or "from inception." "Lack of adequate capital doomed the company to failure *ab initio*." (See AB ORIGINE and AB OVO.)

ab intra
ahb IHN-trah
from within

The insider's role is played out *ab intra*. "The only hope for reform of an institution is through effort expended *ab intra*."

ab irato
ahb ih-RAH-toh
unfair, unprovoked

This phrase may be taken literally as "from an angry man." Thus, any action taken *ab irato* is to be understood as arising from anger rather than reason, and responses to such actions will be weighed carefully by reasonable people. "Orders to fire subordinates were given *ab irato*, and therefore were not carried out until the President had a chance to reconsider."

ab origine
ahb aw-RIH-gih-neh
from the first

Ab origine may be translated as "from the very beginning, source, or origin." The English word "aborigine"—the preferred form is "aboriginal"—comes directly from this phrase and means "original or earliest known inhabitant of a place." "Scholars who are interested in gaining full understanding of an institution, for example, find it valuable to pursue *ab origine* studies in the hope that knowledge of the beginnings of an institution under study will shed light on its present status." (See AB INITIO and AB OVO.)

ab ovo
ahb OH-woh
from the very beginning

The literal meaning of *ab ovo* is "from the egg," so a thorough search is a search *ab ovo*, a thorough analysis is an analysis *ab ovo*, and a complete presentation is one made *ab ovo*. It is interesting to note, however, that *ab ovo* may imply a tedious thoroughness: "Once again we were subjected to a sententious *ab ovo* account that lasted more than an hour and lulled most of us to sleep." (See AB INITIO and AB ORIGINE.)

ab ovo usque ad mala
ahb OH-woh UUS-kweh ahd MAH-lah
from start to finish

A colorful Roman phrase reminiscent of our own "from soup to nuts," since it is literally translated as "from the egg to the apples," but with a meaning that is quite different. "From soup to nuts" refers to completeness, for example, of a multicourse dinner or a Sears Roebuck catalogue. *Ab ovo usque ad mala*, by contrast, means "from start to finish." The expression derives from the fact that Roman dinners often began with eggs and ended with fruit. "Your plan was inadequate *ab ovo usque ad mala* and had no chance for success."

absit invidia
AHB-siht ihn-WIH-dee-ah
no offense intended

When we say *absit invidia*, literally "let ill will be absent," our words reflect the power that Romans attributed to animosity, whether or not openly expressed. They believed, as do many people today, that ill feelings toward someone could cause that person great harm, so they absolved themselves of the intention to harm someone by saying *absit invidia*—the English expressions "no offense" and "no offense intended," by comparison, are mere social gestures intended to prevent ill feelings. *Absit invidia* may also be extended: **absit invidia verbo** (WEHR-boh) means "may it be said without giving offense." (See ABSIT OMEN.)

absit omen
AHB-siht OH-men
may this not be an omen

The rough equivalent of "Protect me, O Lord," *absit omen*, literally "may the omen be absent," was used to invoke divine protection against evil when something foreboding occurred. The Romans, strong believers in divination, employed soothsayers to interpret omens as a means of foretelling the future. Soothsayers were so popular that the Romans had many words for these practitioners, among them **auspex** (OW-speks) and **haruspex** (HAH-ruu-speks). An **auspex** relied on observation of the behavior of birds to foretell the future, and we are indebted to this highly specialized word for our own words "auspices" and "auspicious." A *haruspex* found special value in examining the entrails of sacrificial animals to foretell the future, but also made interpretations based on less gory activities, such as observation of lightning and other natural phenomena. While we do not pay as much attention to omens today, there are those who may say *absit omen* or its equivalent—"knock on wood"?—when a black cat crosses in front of them.

absolvo
ahb-SAWL-woh
I acquit

A judge acquitting a person after a trial may say, "*Absolvo!*" The term may also be used ironically by persons other than judges. For example, a domestic contretemps may end with one of the parties to the dispute using *absolvo* to close the discussion. On the other hand, this use of *absolvo* may protract the conflict.

ab uno disce omnes
ahb OO-noh DIS-keh AWM-nays
from one example learn about all

This maxim, literally "from one learn all," found in Virgil's *Aeneid*, applies to situations in which the import of a single observation is universally applicable. It is careless application of *ab uno disce omnes* that may trap us in faulty generalizations.

ab urbe condita
ahb UUR-beh KAWN-dih-tah
since the founding of the city

Abbreviated **A.U.C.** The city referred to is ancient Rome, the Big Apple of its day. Romans dated years from the founding of their city, in 753 B.C. Tradition has it that in that year Romulus and his twin brother, Remus, built Rome. In infancy the twins were thrown into the Tiber, the river still running through modern Rome, but were saved by a shepherd and suckled by a wolf. Romulus became the first king of Rome upon its founding. Remus was put to death because he mocked his brother's city. *Ab urbe condita* is also given as **anno urbis conditae** (AHN-noh UUR-bis KAWN-dih-tī), "in the year of the founding of the city," also abbreviated **A.U.C.**

abusus non tollit usum
ahb-OO-suus nohn TAWL-lit OO-suum
misuse does not nullify proper use

Broadly applied, this maxim teaches that the value of a procedure, an object, etc., is not destroyed by improper use. The helicopter, for example, was thought of by its principal inventor as a lifesaving machine. If *abusus non tollit usum* is correct, the machine's use in war does not mean the helicopter itself is evil. The value of television as an instructional medium, to take another example, is not destroyed by those who watch the tube all day long. In yet another sense, the maxim may be applied by prescriptive linguists to what they construe as corruptions in usage. *Abusus non tollit usum* for them means that improper use of a word does not destroy its proper use, and those who deal imprecisely with the language are not given carte blanche to work their destructive ways. Recognizing the Latin maxim, Eric Partridge entitled one of his works on language *Usage and*

Abusage. There is another form of *abusus non tollit usum*, which is recognized by jurists as conveying that same thought: **ab abusu ad usum non valet consequentia** (ahb ahb-OO-soo ahd OO-suum nohn WAH-let KAWN-seh-KWEN-tee-ah), "the consequences of abuse do not apply to general use," suggesting that a right should not be withheld because some people abuse it.

abyssus abyssum invocat

ah-BIHS-suus ah-BIHS-suum IHN-waw-kaht

one misstep leads to another

A warning, literally "hell calls hell," in the Psalms of David and a typically Roman maxim as well. In *The Screwtape Letters*, C. S. Lewis said: "The safest road to Hell is the gradual one— the gentle slope, soft underfoot, without sudden turnings, without milestones, without signposts." We can easily see that the first cigarette, the first drink of whiskey, the first step down any inviting path, is difficult to prevent, yet we must always be on guard: *Abyssus abyssum invocat*.

a capite ad calcem

ah KAH-pih-teh ahd KAHL-kehm

thoroughly

Literally "from head to heel," *a capite ad calcem* may be thought of as the Latin equivalent of "from top to bottom" or "from stem to stern." "The candidate, claiming that the entire municipal government was rotten, promised a reorganization *a capite ad calcem*."

accessit

ahk-KEH-siht

honorable mention

This word literally means "he (or she) came near," but in academic settings, particularly in European universities, an *accessit* (pronounced ak-SES-it in English) is the recognition awarded the runner-up in a competition for a medal or other honor. Academic terminology still relies to a great extent on Latin. This is not surprising, since the earliest universities were concerned primarily with, and conducted their official business in, classical languages. *Accessit* has a certain cachet: "I had hoped to win first prize, but I knew I would be content with an *accessit*" is far more comforting than "close but no cigar" or even "honorable mention."

Acheruntis pabulum
AH-keh-RUUN-tihs PAH-boo-luum
food for the gallows

Acheruntis pabulum should not be applied willy-nilly to all the poor wretches who sit on death row, but only to those who may be thought of as deserving to die. Acheron—the Romans called it **Acheruns** (AH-keh-ruuns)—was one of seven rivers said to flow around Hell. Thus, any person adjudged sufficiently evil may be said to be *Acheruntis pabulum*, literally "food of Acheron."

a cruce salus
ah KROO-keh SAH-luus
salvation (comes) from the cross

The cross is, of course, the symbol of the death of Christ, and Christ's death meant redemption for his followers. Thus, *a cruce salus* is the teaching that salvation comes from belief in Christianity.

acta est fabula
AHK-tah ehst FAH-buu-lah
it's all over

In the classical theater, with no curtain to draw across the stage, the words *acta est fabula*, literally "the drama has been acted out," signified the end of a performance. In another context, Emperor Augustus is said to have uttered *"Acta est fabula"* just before he died, establishing a pattern followed by Rabelais, whose last words are said to have been *"La farce est jouée,"* "the farce is ended." *Acta est fabula* may be spoken appropriately whenever a life or an unfolding event comes to an unhappy end, or one could say, "It's curtains."

acta sanctorum
AHK-tah sahn-KTOH-ruum
deeds of the saints

Accounts of the lives of the Christian martyrs and saints are used in teaching the faith. The most famous collection is the monumental *Acta Sanctorum*, initiated by the Bollandists, a group named for Jean Bolland, the seventeenth-century Flemish Jesuit, and in English usually called *Lives of the Saints*. This great work, still the responsibility of the Bollandists, is arranged according to the dates of the ecclesiastical calendar. It is approaching seventy volumes in length and still growing.

ad absurdum
ahd ahb-SUUR-duum
to absurdity

See REDUCTIO AD ABSURDUM.

ad arbitrium
ahd ahr-BIH-tree-uum
at pleasure

Anything done of one's own will is performed *ad arbitrium*. "In this life, how many actions are really taken *ad arbitrium*?" Another expression for the same thought is **arbitrio suo** (ahr-BIH-tree-oh SOO-oh), "on his (or her) own authority."

ad astra per aspera
ahd AH-strah per AH-speh-rah
to the stars through difficulties

The motto of Kansas, teaching us that we achieve great things only by encountering and overcoming adversity.

ad augusta per angusta
ahd ow-GUU-stah per ahn-GUU-stah
to honors through difficulties

Augusta refers to holy places, *angusta* to narrow spaces. This maxim tells us, therefore, that we cannot achieve great results without suffering, the suffering being represented here by squeezing through narrow spaces. A fit motto for dieters.

ad calendas graecas
ahd kah-LEN-dahs GRĪ-kahs
never

The literal translation of this Roman version of "when hell freezes over" is "at the Greek calends." The rub is that the calends, the first day of the month, was a feature of the Roman calendar, and the Greeks had no calends. It was on the calends that interest on borrowed money was to be paid, so for Roman debtors they were **tristes calendae** (TRIH-stays kah-LEN-dī), "the unhappy calends."

ad captandum vulgus
ahd kah-PTAHN-duum WUUL-guus
in order to win over the masses

Actions taken *ad captandum vulgus* are intended to please the common people. The implication is that such actions may not be in the best interest of society, but are intended only to achieve popularity. Politicians campaigning for office, for example, are wont to promise reforms *ad captandum vulgus* and never give a thought to accomplishing them.

ad clerum
ahd KLEH-ruum
to the clergy

A statement made by a church leader and intended only for the ears of the clergy is made *ad clerum*, as opposed to a statement **ad populum** (ahd PAW-puu-luum), "to the people."

a Deo et Rege
ah DEH-oh et REH-geh
from God and the King

Divine monarchs saw themselves as representatives of God on earth, so documents issued by them were often signed *a Deo et Rege*.

Adeste Fideles
ahd-EH-steh fih-DAY-lays
O come, all ye faithful

A Christmas hymn written in Latin, date and author uncertain.

ad eundem gradum
ahd eh-UUN-dem GRAH-duum
to the same degree

Often abbreviated **ad eundem**, this phrase can be used to apportion blame or praise justly among parties to a deed. "The judge held both litigants accountable *ad eundem*." *Ad eundem gradum* has a special use when applied to academic life. Construing *gradum* as an academic rank, under special circumstances a student holding a Master of Arts degree from one university may be awarded the same degree by another university without examination, such degree being termed "M.A. *ad eundem gradum*."

ad gloriam
ahd GLAW-ree-ahm
for glory

See AD MAIOREM DEI GLORIAM.

ad gustum
ahd GUU-stuum
to one's taste

A cookbook expression. "Add salt *ad gustum*."

ad hoc
ahd hawk
for this (purpose)

An *ad hoc* (pronounced ad HOK in English) committee is a temporary committee established to accomplish a particular task. Once an *ad hoc* committee has completed the job for which it was established, it is disbanded.

ad hominem
ahd HAW-mih-nem
against the man

See AD REM and ARGUMENTUM AD HOMINEM.

adhuc sub iudice (or judice) lis est
AHD-huuk suub YOO-dih-keh lees est
the case is still before the court

Members of the legal profession are enjoined from public discussion of any matters that are under adjudication (*sub iudice*). People under indictment and public officials accused of misconduct in office may invoke *adhuc sub iudice lis est* as a means of avoiding public discussion of their problems.

ad infinitum
ahd ihn-fee-NEE-tuum
without limit

Abbreviated **ad inf.** and **ad infin.**, this phrase is the Latin equivalent of "forever, to infinity, endlessly," and in English is pronounced ad in-fə-NĪT-əm. "Her husband went on *ad infinitum* on the question of equal division of household chores." (See AD NAUSEAM.)

ad interim
ahd IHN-teh-rim
in the meantime

This phrase, which has an English counterpart, "in the interim," is often abbreviated **ad int.**

ad kalendas graecas
ahd kah-LEN-dahs GRĪ-kahs
never

Alternative spelling for AD CALENDAS GRAECAS.

ad libitum
ahd LIH-bih-tuum
extemporaneously

Literally meaning "at pleasure" and abbreviated **ad lib.** in Latin, this expression is popularly used as a noun phrase or modifier in English in the form "ad lib" to express absence of planning. "His worst jokes were carefully planned ad libs."

ad limina apostolorum
ahd LEE-mih-nah ah-PAW-staw-LOH-ruum
to the highest authority

This expression, literally "to the thresholds of the Apostles," is applied to matters appropriate for papal consideration and disposition before the tombs of St. Peter and St. Paul. Often abbreviated **ad limina,** the expression finds its widest use in more mundane applications: "The chairman of the Romance Languages Department suggested that the committee was beyond its authority and that the matter be taken *ad limina.*" In such a case, the question would surely be settled by higher campus authority.

ad litem
ahd LEE-tem
for the suit or action

Among lawyers, an *ad litem* decision is taken as valid only for the lis (lees), the controversy under adjudication. Thus, a guardian *ad litem* is appointed by a court to act for a minor only in regard to the problem of the minor before the court, not to serve as a substitute father.

ad litteram (also literam)
ahd LIHT-teh-rahm
to the last jot

Littera has as one of its meanings "letter of the alphabet." *Ad litteram*, literally "to the letter," means "precisely." "We must live up to our agreement *ad litteram.*"

ad locum
ahd LOH-kuum
at or to the place

Abbreviated **ad loc.**

ad maiorem Dei gloriam

ahd mah-YAW-rem DEH-ee GLAW-ree-ahm

for the greater glory of God

Motto of the Society of Jesuits. The abbreviation **A.M.D.G.** appears as an epigraph in books produced by the Jesuit order. The full expression is sometimes cited as the rationale for actions taken by any Christians.

ad nauseam

ahd NOW-seh-ahm

to the point of (causing) nausea

Anything unpleasurable that appears to go on endlessly may be said to be proceeding *ad nauseam*, literally "to seasickness." The clear meaning of this phrase, in English pronounced ad NAW-zee-əm, is that such activity has reached the point at which it is almost more than a body can bear. Nothing that gives pleasure can properly be described in this way. "The lecturer went on *ad nauseam*, apparently determined to read to us every last word in his notes."

ad patres

ahd PAH-trays

dead

The literal translation of *ad patres* is "to the fathers" or "to the ancestors." To go *ad patres* is to die; to send someone *ad patres* is to kill that person.

ad perpetuam rei memoriam

ahd per-PET-oo-ahm REH-ee me-MAW-ree-ahm

for the perpetual remembrance of the thing

Words traditionally used to open papal bulls.

ad populum
ahd PAW-puu-luum
to the people

Populus means "the entire people." An *ad populum* statement is one intended for the ears of the masses.

ad praesens ova cras pullis sunt meliora
ahd PRĪ-sens OH-wah krahs PUU-lees suunt me-lee-OH-rah
a bird in the hand is worth two in the bush

This conservative maxim translates literally as "eggs today are better than chickens tomorrow." The advice is appropriate for all who take risks, e.g., stockbrokers' clients and crapshooters: It is usually more prudent to hold on to what one has than to risk everything in speculation.

ad quem
ahd kwem
for (or to) which (or whom)

ad quod damnum
ahd kwawd DAHM-nuum
to what damage

A legal writ used for assessing damages relating to land taken for public use.

ad referendum
ahd reh-feh-REHN-duum
for further consideration

Ad referendum, which translates literally as "for referring," is a diplomats' term. Diplomats who accept a proposal for their governments *ad referendum* indicate by their actions that final acceptance is dependent on the approval of the diplomats' governments. *Referendum* has come over directly into English with the meaning of "a vote by all qualified voters on a matter of public concern."

ad rem
ahd rem
to the matter at hand

Ad rem, literally "to the thing," can be rendered in various ways. With the meaning "pertinent" or "relevant": "The attorney was admonished to make only *ad rem* comments or be silent." "In a straightforward manner": "Because of the limitation on debate, it is vital to speak *ad rem* if we are to conclude our considerations within the allotted time." Above all, it must be noted that *ad rem* is the phrase that contrasts with AD HOMINEM. Debaters who argue *ad rem* address the matter at hand to score points in the debate; debaters who argue *ad hominem* attack their opponents to score points.

adsum
AHD-suum
present!

A formal answer to a roll call, literally "I am here."

ad unguem
ahd UUN-gwem
perfectly

This phrase, literally "to a fingernail," is used to convey the thought of accomplishing something well or precisely. A sculptor in ancient times would test the smoothness of a finished surface by running a fingernail over it.

ad unum omnes
ahd OO-nuum AWM-nays

unanimously

Literally "all to one." "The delegates accepted the resolution *ad unum omnes*."

ad usum Delphini
ahd OO-suum del-FEE-nee

expurgated

A modern Latin phrase, translated literally as "for the Dauphin's use." An edition of classic works prepared for the Dauphin, heir to the throne of Louis XIV of France, carried the title *Ad usum Delphini*. The works, as might be expected, were expurgated to avoid offending the royal young man, so any expurgated work today may be termed *ad usum Delphini*.

ad utrumque paratus
ahd oo-TRUUM-kweh pah-RAH-tuus

prepared for the worst

A mature person is ready to cope with any eventuality, including the final one. The Romans described such a person as *ad utrumque paratus*, literally "ready for either (eventuality)." (See SEMPER PARATUS.)

ad valorem
ahd wah-LOH-rem

in proportion to value

Abbreviated **ad val.** An import duty fixed *ad valorem* is one established on the basis of the commercial value of the imported item. Like death and taxes, *ad valorem* has been with us so long that it now is part of the English language and pronounced ad və-LOH-rəm.

ad verbum
ahd WEHR-buum
verbatim

The phrase *ad verbum*, literally "to the word," is the Roman equivalent of the English "verbatim," which is a direct borrowing from medieval Latin. (See VERBATIM ET LITTERATIM.) The Romans had several other expressions for "word-for-word": **e verbo, de verbo,** and **pro verbo.** Perhaps this tells us something about the difficulty of making accurate copies before printing was invented.

adversa
ahd-WEHR-sah
things noted

A scholarly expression referring to observations one has made.

adversaria
ahd-wehr-SAH-ree-ah
a journal

Adversaria, literally "that which has been turned to," is a plural noun referring to notes or brief written comments. "Her *adversaria* were fascinating in their perceptions." It also refers to annotations or commentaries written on a facing page of a book. As a singular noun, an *adversaria* (English pronunciation ad-vər-SA-ree-ə) is a journal or commonplace book, a book used for recording one's observations as well as for collecting poems, brief essays, and any other material one finds worth keeping.

adversus solem ne loquitor
ahd-WEHR-suus SOH-lem nay LOH-kwih-tawr
don't waste your time arguing the obvious

This maxim advises one literally, "don't speak against the sun." When confronted by an all-important, irrefutable fact, there is no point in disputing further. The smoking gun, the telltale blond hair, the lipstick smudge, all signal the end of the discussion for any reasonable culprit: it is time for plea bargaining. (See IN FLAGRANTE DELICTO.)

ad vitam
ahd WEE-tahm
for life

A legal term sometimes found in wills, with the meaning of "for use during a person's life only." (See AD VITAM AUT CULPAM.)

ad vitam aeternam
ahd WEE-tahm ī-TEHR-nahm
forever

Ad vitam aeternam, literally "for eternal life," conveys the idea of "for all time." "Here is the money, but know that this is payment *ad vitam aeternam*."

ad vitam aut culpam
ahd WEE-tahm owt KUUL-pahm
for life or until a misdeed

The origin of *ad vitam aut culpam* rests in the feudal practice of conveying property or privilege that would not revert to the grantor until the death or misbehavior of the person receiving the benefit. One can see that such a grant might impose discipline on the recipient to behave properly or risk loss of the beneficence. Today, any gift given with strings attached, such as an automobile to one's son on condition that he drive it safely, might be said to be made *ad vitam aut culpam*.

advocatus diaboli
ahd-waw-KAH-tuus dee-AH-baw-lee
devil's advocate

The Roman Catholic Church uses the term **promotor fidei** (proh-MOH-tawr fih-DEH-ee), "promoter of the faith," or *advocatus diaboli*, to designate the church official appointed to argue against a proposed canonization or beatification. It is this official's responsibility to find the flaws in the evidence presented by those who support the proposed designation of the **beatus** (beh-AH-tuus), "the blessed person." In this trial of opposing forces, it is expected that the truth will emerge to support or deny canonization. A person playing devil's advocate today is too often a person fond of taking the unpopular side of any issue under discussion, and primarily for the sake of argument.

aeger
Ī-gehr
sick

In Latin, *aeger* as a noun means "an invalid"; as an adjective it means "sick." In British universities, *aeger* (Ī-jər) is the traditional term used on students' medical excuses for failing to appear for an examination, and a medical excuse itself may also be called an *aeger*. (See AEGROTAT.)

aegrescit medendo
ī-GREH-skit meh-DEN-doh
the remedy is worse than the disease

Aegrescit medendo, Virgil's phrase, literally means "the disease worsens with the treatment." Those who question the efficacy of some medical treatment may use this phrase appropriately as their battle cry.

aegri somnia
Ī-gree SAW-mnee-ah
a sick man's dreams

An *aegri somnia*, Horace's phrase, may be translated more freely as "a hallucination." "They tend to treat everything I say as an *aegri somnia*." The Romans appear to have been acutely aware of the role of the emotions in causing symptoms of illness. Virgil spoke of **aegra amans** (Ī-grah AH-mahns), "lover's disease," and Livy spoke of **aeger amore** (Ī-ger ah-MOH-reh) to describe the same condition, in apt recognition of the pathology of romance.

aegrotat
ī-GROH-taht
a note from the doctor

Aegrotat literally means "he (or she) is sick." Thus, in British universities, an *aegrotat* (Ī-groh-tat) is an official medical excuse. (See AEGER.) But the meaning extends beyond that. An *aegrotat* is also an unclassified degree that may be granted by a British university to a student who completes all academic requirements save final examinations, if the student is too sick to sit for the examinations.

aequam servare mentem
Ī-kwahm ser-WAH-reh MEN-tem
to keep one's cool

Aequam servare mentem, which translates literally as "to keep an unruffled mind," recognizes the value of maintaining a clear head while conducting the business of life, especially when making important decisions. Horace, in his *Odes*, suggested **aequam memento rebus in arduis** (meh-MEN-toh REH-buus ihn AHR-duu-ees) **servare mentem**, adjuring us to remember to maintain a clear head when attempting difficult tasks.

aequo animo
Ī-kwoh AH-nih-moh
calmly

Aequo animo, literally "with a calm mind," refers to evenness of mental attitude. Anyone who has composure or equanimity usually behaves *aequo animo*.

aere perennius
Ī-re peh-REN-nee-uus
everlasting

The Romans, who knew the characteristics of certain metals, used the word **aes** (īs) for copper and its alloys, brass and bronze. When, therefore, they wished to respond to someone who had done a favor, they might use *aere perennius*, literally "more durable than bronze," to suggest that the friendship shown would last forever. Certainly a more felicitous response than "I owe you one."

aetatis suae
ī-TAH-tihs SOO-ī
of his (or her) age

Aetatis alone means "of the age," while *aetatis suae* means "in a particular year of one's life." Tombstones once carried such inscriptions as "Died *aetatis suae* 37," or "A.S. 37." *Aetatis suae* is also given as **anno** (AH-noh) **aetatis suae**, meaning "in the year of his (or her) age."

aeternum vale
ī-TEHR-nuum WAH-lay
farewell forever

A suitable inscription for a tombstone, perhaps also a suitable phrase to use when ending a love affair.

a fortiori
ah fawr-tee-OH-ree
with stronger reason

A *fortiori* may be interpreted as meaning "even more certain" or "all the more." Thus we can say: "If you refuse to trust him with the petty cash box, *a fortiori* you must not let him handle our bank deposits."

a fronte praecipitium a tergo lupi
ah FRAWN-teh prī-kih-PIH-tee-uum ah TEHR-goh LOO-pee
between a rock and a hard place

A *fronte praecipitium a tergo lupi* is literally "a precipice in front, wolves behind." What to do when caught between equally hazardous or difficult alternatives or, as we once said, "between the devil and the deep blue sea"?

age quod agis
AH-geh kwawd AH-gihs
pay attention to what you are doing

Age quod agis, literally "do what you are doing," is excellent advice for those who become careless in their work as well as for those who fail to do what they are supposed to do.

Agnus Dei
AH-gnuus DEH-ee
Lamb of God

Agnus Dei, the epithet applied to Christ by John the Baptist, is represented in the figure of a lamb supporting a cross or a banner with a cross emblazoned on it. The lamb, often shown with a halo about its head, represents Christ. A medallion stamped with this figure and blessed by the Pope is also an *Agnus Dei*. The words *Agnus Dei*, translated as "O Lamb of

God," are heard in the office for burial of the dead in the Catholic mass, and the music for this part of the service is called an *Agnus Dei*.

a latere
ah LAH-tehr-eh
from the side

Cardinals in the particular confidence of a pope—having the ear of the pope—are said to be *a latere* cardinals. A papal emissary enjoying such confidence is called **legatus** (leh-GAH-tuus) **a latere**. In a broader sense, any person who is a close adviser to an important official can be given the informal appellation *a latere*, implying power for the adviser and status for the official. In government, a plenipotentiary may be thought of as a *legatus a latere*. *A latere* is also used in law, with the meaning "collateral," in describing succession to property.

albae gallinae filius
AHL-bī gahl-LEE-nī FEE-lee-uus
a lucky devil

Albae gallinae filius, literally "a son of a white hen," found its meaning in a Roman folk tale. An eagle was said to have dropped a white hen into the lap of Livia, the wife of Emperor Augustus. This remarkable incident was interpreted by soothsayers as a favorable omen, since white hens were believed to bring good fortune. We refer to a particular type of lucky fellow as someone "born with a silver spoon in his mouth," and the phrase *albae gallinae filius* may be used in this sense as well.

albo lapillo notare diem
AHL-boh lah-PIHL-loh noh-TAH-reh DEE-em
to mark a day with a white stone

Colors have symbolic meanings in all cultures. For the Romans, white was the symbol of happiness, black of misfortune.

Thus, in a trial a vote for acquittal was cast with a white stone, for condemnation, a black one; and a happy day was marked with a white stone, an unhappy day with a black one. The latter procedure was this: At the end of each day, a Roman—according to Pliny the Younger, this superstitious practice dated back to the Thracians—would judge whether the day had been happy or unhappy. Once decided, the Roman would drop a pebble of the appropriate color into an urn, so at the end of a month he could empty the urn and be able to look back over the month past. (See NIGRO NOTANDA LAPILLO.) We still speak of red-letter days, so why not an *albo lapillo*, a white-stone day?

alea iacta est
AH-lay-ah YAH-ktah est
the die is cast

Julius Caesar, preparing in 49 B.C. to enter Rome from Gaul, where he was governor, came to the Rubicon, the river that marked the boundary between Cisalpine Gaul and Italy. Caesar knew that once he crossed the Rubicon he would be in great danger, since he would be seen as defying his government. Suetonius reported that Caesar, anxious over the possible effects of the move he was considering, on the night before making his decision saw an apparition that impelled him to take the warlike step. (Plutarch gave a different account. According to Plutarch, on the night before the crossing, Caesar was so troubled by the gravity of his contemplated action against the mother country that he dreamed he had sexual intercourse with his own mother.) Both sources do agree, however, that when Caesar finally made up his mind to move boldly, he said, "*Iacta alea est*," a common phrase of the time. Even today, "The die is cast" means that a bold and irretrievable decision has been made. Caesar's decision eventually resulted in triumph. Those who know only the English translation of *alea iacta* (or *iacta alea*) *est* may think erroneously that *alea* refers to another kind of "die," rather than the singular form of "dice." It is also worth pointing out that in English, "to cross the Rubicon" is to commit oneself to a hazardous enterprise by taking a decisive action that cannot be undone.

alere flammam
AH-leh-reh FLAH-mahm
to feed the flame

Ovid spoke of **alere flammas**, "to feed the flames," in a figurative sense, which is the intention today whenever we say *alere flammam* or *alere flammas*. "Further discussion on this matter will only serve *alere flammam*." One may also use these phrases when speaking of rekindling feelings of love, ambition, and the like. Old flames never die?

alias dictus
AH-lee-ahs DIH-ktuus
otherwise called

The full ancestor of the English word "alias," with the meaning "an assumed name." As a Latin word, *alias* can be translated as "at another time." While our own use of *alias* usually limits its application to circumstances less than honorable—in contrast with "pen name" and "stage name"—the Romans did not intend this. They used *alias dictus* in referring to someone's nickname, employed without any interest in deception. In modern law, the expression may be used in much the same way as "also known as" (abbreviated **a.k.a.**) is employed. "Schmidt *alias dictus* Smith owned the business for only two months."

alieni generis
ah-lee-AY-nee GEH-neh-rihs
of a different kind

alieni iuris (or juris)
ah-lee-AY-nee YUU-rihs
subject to another's authority

Alieni iuris, a term in law, literally means "of another's law." When, for example, a court places an infant (someone below the legal age of maturity) or a mentally incompetent person under control of a guardian, the infant or incompetent person is said to be *alieni iuris*. Those who are *alieni iuris* cannot exercise control of their ordinary legal rights, but must submit to the authority of appointed guardians.

aliquando bonus dormitat Homerus
ah-lih-KWAHN-doh BOH-nuus DAWR-mih-taht
hoh-MAY-ruus
you can't win 'em all

A modification, literally "sometimes even good Homer dozes," of Horace's line concerning Homer (see QUANDOQUE BONUS DORMITAT HOMERUS). The intention is that even the best of writers do not always knock us out, or more broadly, even the greatest in any field are not always up to form. This is said to excuse one's own less than perfect efforts or to criticize gently the work of another that is not up to usual quality.

alis volat propriis
AH-lees WAW-laht PROH-pree-ees
she (he) flies on her (his) own wings

Motto of Oregon. The intention is clear: Oregonians are proud of their ability to get along on their own. Anyone who has the same independent spirit can also adopt this motto. In line with today's enlightened parenthood, a parent watching proudly as a child manages independently can say *alis volat propriis*. The Latin gives no indication of gender, so the statement can be made of any newly independent offspring. The translation "she flies on her own wings" reflects the customs of a less enlightened day, when gender was applied to ships of state as well as to other ships. (For the crossword puzzle fan, it is worth mentioning that **ala** (AH-lah) means "wing.")

alma mater
AHL-mah MAH-tehr
nourishing mother

Alma mater is the epithet applied by Romans to Ceres, goddess of growing vegetation; to Cybele, a nature goddess; and to other bounteous goddesses. Roman poets referred to the country of their birth as *alma mater*. Today, the expression is used to refer to one's college or university, and more narrowly, to the official song, statue, or other symbol of the institution. Columbia University, just one of many, has a large statue of Alma Mater (in English AL-mə MAH-tər) standing in front of its administration building, and this statue is a favorite background for snapshots taken by proud parents of entering freshmen. The symbolism is clear: The university is the bounteous, fostering mother of all its graduates. (See ALUMNUS.)

alter ego
AHL-tehr EH-goh
bosom pal

Literally translated as "another I" or "another self," an *alter ego* is an inseparable friend. The intention is that an alter ego (English pronunciation, awl-tər EE-goh) may be considered as speaking or acting for the other person. Another way of conveying the same thought is given in the next phrase, ALTER IDEM, which is far less common.

alter idem
AHL-tehr EE-dem
another self

Cicero used the expression **tamquam** (TAHM-kwahm) **alter idem**, "as if a second self," to describe a completely trustworthy friend, an ALTER EGO. *Idem* means "the same," while *ego* means "I," but both phrases convey the same meaning. Anyone who is your *alter idem* or *alter ego* is your inseparable friend.

altissima quaeque flumina minimo sono labi
ahl-TIH-sih-ɪnah KWĪ-kweh FLOO-mih-nah
MIH-nih-moh SOH-noh LAH-bee
still waters run deep

Literally "the deepest rivers flow with the least sound," this Roman proverb suggests that we not sell short those who eschew self-promotion, at the same time cautioning us to watch out for people given to blowing their own horns.

alumnus
ah-LUU-mnuus
nursling, foster child

We all know the English word "alumnus" as a graduate or former student of an academic institution, and even of an institution not commonly thought of as academic, so it is interesting to understand the Latin *alumnus*, with the meanings given above. When we understand *alumnus* in its Roman intention, we can better understand the idea of ALMA MATER as "nourishing mother." It is also worthwhile to discuss other forms of the word *alumnus*. The plural of *alumnus* is **alumni** (ah-LUU-mnee; in English, ə-LUM-nī). The feminine of *alumnus* is **alumna** (ah-LUU-mnah; in English, ə-LUM-nə). The feminine plural is **alumnae** (ah-LUU-mnī; in English, ə-LUM-nee or ə-LUM-nī). Clear?

amantes sunt amentes
ah-MAHN-tays suunt ah-MEHN-tays
lovers are lunatics

The foolish things that lovers do are considered justification for this maxim. In *A Midsummer Night's Dream*, Shakespeare's Theseus puts it thus:

> The lunatic, the lover, and the poet
> Are of imagination all compact.

Those of us who still have our wits will take this into account when we are smitten. After all, Publilius Syrus advised us that **amare et sapere vix deo conceditur** (ah-MAH-reh et SAH-peh-reh weeks DAY-oh kawn-KAY-dih-tuur), "even a god finds it hard to love and be wise at the same time."

amantium irae amoris integratio est
ah-MAHN-tee-uum IH-rī ah-MOH-rihs
ihn-teh-GRAH-tee-oh est
lovers' quarrels are the renewal of love

How much truth there is in this old Roman proverb is anyone's guess, but Terence is the source for this insight, and others have picked it up. Robert Frost said in one poem that he would choose as an epitaph: "I had a lover's quarrel with the world." What better way to express one's love affair with life? (See QUI BENE AMAT BENE CASTIGAT for further wisdom.)

a maximis ad minima
ah MAH-ksih-mees ahd MIH-nih-mah
from the greatest to the least

This expression refers to objects or abstractions, not people. "She concerned herself with all of society's problems, *a maximis ad minima*."

a mensa et toro
ah MEN-sah et TAW-roh
a legal separation

A mensa et toro, with the literal meaning of "from table and bed," is found in the legal phrase "divorce *a mensa et toro*," referring to a decree forbidding husband and wife to share living quarters. *Mensa* is translated in this construction as "a table for dining," but it also means "altar" or "sacrificial table" in other uses, as well as "a table used by moneychangers" for doing their business. Those with a cynical attitude toward marriage and divorce thus might well read cruel humor into a divorce *a mensa et toro*. Even more ironic is the meaning of torus (TAW-ruus), from which we have the form *toro*. *Torus* has many meanings, one of which is "bed" and another, "marriage couch," but in other contexts it carries the meaning of "bier."

amicus curiae
ah-MEE-kuus KOO-ree-ī
an impartial spokesman in a court of law

An *amicus curiae*, literally "friend of the court," is a person not party to a litigation who volunteers or is invited by the court to give advice on a matter pending before it. Currently, several organizations, in particular the American Civil Liberties Union, appear regularly as **amici** (ah-MEE-kee) **curiae** (plural of *amicus curiae*) in cases that interest them.

amicus humani generis
ah-MEE-kuus hoo-MAH-nee GEH-neh-rihs
a philanthropist

Literally "a friend of the human race."

amicus usque ad aras
ah-MEE-kuus UU-skweh ahd AH-rahs
a friend to the end

Literally "a friend as far as to the altars," this expression can be taken as "a friend unto death," but it is also interpreted as "a friend up to the point where friendship conflicts with religious or ethical beliefs." Pericles of Athens is said to have responded in this latter sense when refusing to swear falsely for a friend.

amor

AH-mawr

love

The word used to express fondness or passion. (See the next four entries.)

amor nummi

AH-mawr NUUM-mee

cupidity

Literally "love of money." (See RADIX OMNIUM MALORUM EST CUPIDITAS.)

amor patriae

AH-mawr PAH-tree-ī

patriotism

Literally "love of country."

amor proximi

AH-mawr PRAW-ksih-mee

love of one's neighbor

Leviticus adjures "love thy neighbor as thyself." At the same time, we must be careful not to covet our neighbor's wife.

amor vincit omnia

AH-mawr WIHN-kiht AWM-nee-ah

love conquers all

This famous line of Virgil's (also given, to the despair of beginning Latin students, unaccustomed to the flexibility of Latin word order, as **amor omnia vincit** or as **omnia vincit amor**) is quoted by Chaucer in the "Prologue" to *The Canterbury Tales.*

Incidentally, Virgil goes on to say, **et nos cedamus amori** (et nohs keh-DAHM-uus ah-MAWR-ee), "and let us yield to it [love]."

anguis in herba
AHN-gwihs ihn HEHR-bah
a hidden danger

Literally "a snake in the grass." Virgil, in his *Eclogues*, used the expression **latet** (LAH-tet) **anguis in herba**, "a snake lies concealed in the grass," to call attention to a hidden danger. The danger may be of any type, even though the English "snake in the grass" is usually a person who has turned against his friend, particularly an adulterer who has taken up with the friend's wife.

animal bipes implume
AHN-ih-mahl BIH-pays ihm-PLOO-may
a human being

Literally "a two-legged animal without feathers," *animal bipes implume* is the Latin translation of Plato's definition of man, and thus a contemptuous designation for **Homo sapiens** (literally "wise man," itself a world-class self-serving expression). Two other uses of *animal* are worthy of note here. **Animal disputans** (DIH-spuu-tahns) is "an argumentative person," and **animal rationale** (rah-tee-oh-NAH-leh) is "a reasoning person," and like *animal bipes implume*, both may be translated as "a human being."

animis opibusque parati
AH-nih-mees OH-pih-BUUS-kweh pah-RAH-tee
ready for anything

Literally meaning "prepared in minds and resources," this upbeat saying is one of two mottoes of South Carolina. The other is DUM SPIRO SPERO, "where there's life there's hope."

Any prudent person is always *animis opibusque parati*, but this saying has special application for those who embark on a new adventure, and it may also serve those who anticipate the unpredictable final adventure of all mortals, as any life insurance salesman will tell you. Thus, South Carolina pictures itself as prudent in the one motto and tenacious in the other. No wonder nothing could be finer than to be in Carolina.

anno aetatis suae . . .

AHN-noh ī-TAH-tihs SOO-ī

in the year of his (or her) age . . .

This is the full expression often given as AETATIS SUAE. It is seen on tombstones as well as in old texts and family Bibles, often abbreviated A.A.S. "Died A.A.S. 64."

anno Domini

AHN-noh DAW-mih-nee

in the year of our Lord

The full version of the abbreviation **A.D.** Modern Western calendars reckon passage of time from the birth of Christ, the commencement of the Christian era, but there is disagreement over the precise year of Christ's birth. (See the next four entries.)

anno hegirae

AHN-noh HEH-gih-rī

in the year of the hegira

The year A.D. 622 is the year in which Muhammad fled from Mecca to Medina, and the month is generally given as September, so it is A.D. 622 that is taken as the beginning of the Muslim era, the precise date for the first day of the Muslim era corresponding to July 16, 622. The Arabic word for "flight" is *hijirah*, from which came the Latin word **hegira** (HEH-gih-rah) and then the English word "hegira" (hi-JĪ-rə). To commemorate Muhammad's flight, Muslims make the same journey as a pilgrimage. *Anno hegirae* is abbreviated **A.H.** in giving dates in the Muslim calendar. The curious may be gratified to learn that 1421 A.H. will commence early in A.D. 2000.

anno mundi
AHN-noh MUUN-dee
in the year of the world

Yet another term for reckoning passage of time from a fixed event. *Anno mundi*, abbreviated **A.M.**, marks the number of years that have passed since the world began. In the Hebrew tradition, the year of creation corresponds to 3761 B.C. The Irish theologian Ussher in the mid-seventeenth century computed the date of creation as 4004 B.C. Thus, the year A.D. 2000 will correspond to 5761 A.M. or 6004 A.M., depending on whose date of creation is preferred.

anno regni
AHN-noh REHG-nee
in the year of the reign

Abbreviated **A.R.**, *anno regni* is used to mark the passage of years in the reign of a monarch.

anno urbis conditae
AHN-noh UUR-bis KAWN-dih-tī
in the year since Rome was founded

For Romans, "the city," **urbs** (uurbs), was none other than Rome, so *anno urbis conditae*, literally "in the year of the founded city," refers to the number of years that have passed since 753 B.C., the traditional date of the founding of Rome. (See AB URBE CONDITA.)

annuit coeptis

AHN-noo-it koh-AYP-tees

He (God) has favored our undertaking

This saying, from Virgil's *Aeneid*, appears on the reverse of
the great seal of the United States, which can be seen by all but
the most impecunious on the reverse of the United States one-
dollar bill. By employing *annuit coeptis* in this way, we join
many other countries in suggesting that God takes a special
interest in particular societies. (See E PLURIBUS UNUM and
NOVUS ORDO SECLORUM.)

annus mirabilis

AHN-nuus mee-RAH-bih-lihs

a remarkable year

Any year in which great events occur may be called an *annus
mirabilis*, for example, A.D. 1666, when a great fire raged in
London for almost a week and virtually destroyed that city. The
phrase is also used to designate a year in which figures of great
importance were born, particularly when that year produced
important people in great numbers. Thus, the year 1809 is
considered an *annus mirabilis*. Consider first Charles Darwin
and Abraham Lincoln, who were born in that year, and then go
on to Alfred, Lord Tennyson and to Nikolai Gogol, Oliver Wen-
dell Holmes, Edgar Allan Poe, and Felix Mendelssohn, as well
as Louis Braille, Edward FitzGerald, William Gladstone, Fanny
Kemble, Cyrus McCormick, and even Kit Carson—they don't
hardly make years like that one no more.

ante bellum

AHN-teh BEL-luum

before the war

The period before any war may be characterized as *ante
bellum*, but in the United States the phrase generally is applied
to the period before the Civil War. In English, "antebellum"

(ant-i-BEL-əm) is used as an adjective with the meaning "pre-war": "The antebellum South is looked back upon with great nostalgia by some Americans."

ante Christum
AHN-teh KREE-stuum
before Christ

Abbreviated **A.C.** (See ANNO DOMINI.)

ante meridiem
AHN-teh meh-REE-dee-em
before noon

Meridies (meh-REE-dee-ays) means "noon" or "midday." A.M., the English abbreviation for *ante meridiem*, refers to time prior to noon and after midnight. (See POST MERIDIEM.)

ante mortem
AHN-teh MAWR-tem
before death

Ante mortem, abbreviated **A.M.** but not to be confused with ANNO MUNDI or with ANTE MERIDIEM, which have the same abbreviation, is an easily understood phrase that refers to the period in which death is imminent. The phrase has fathered an English adjective, "antemortem" (ant-i-MAWRT-əm): An antemortem statement is a deathbed statement and therefore is given great weight in a court of law, since a person who knows death is near is presumed to have no reason to tell anything but the truth.

ante partum
AHN-teh PAHR-tuum
before childbirth

The period before childbirth may be described as *ante partum*. (See POST PARTUM.)

apage Satanas
AHP-ah-geh SAH-tah-nahs
away with thee, Satan

The concept of Satan as the archfiend is part of the Judeo-Christian tradition. The meaning of the noun *satan* (SAW-tawn) in Hebrew, from which we work through Greek to find our way to *Satanas* in Latin, is "adversary," and we still contend with Satan today. Matthew says: "Get thee behind me, Satan." Today, with a little Latin, anyone confronted by temptation may say, "*Apage Satanas*."

apologia pro vita sua
ah-paw-LAW-gee-ah proh WEE-tah SOO-ah
a defense of his life

An *apologia* (English pronunciation, ap-ə-LOH-jə) is especially a written justification for one's opinions or actions. John Henry Newman, the celebrated Anglican theologian who converted to Catholicism in 1845, wrote *Apologia Pro Vita Sua* (1864), his religious autobiography, in which he defends the things he did in his life by way of explaining the basis for his faith. He was made a cardinal in 1879 and is known usually as Cardinal Newman. Anyone can write an *apologia pro vita sua*, but it is clear that any such attempt will be looked upon as effrontery in light of Cardinal Newman's accomplishment, which is considered a literary masterpiece.

a posteriori
ah PAW-steh-ree-OH-ree
from effect to cause

Reasoning *a posteriori*, literally "from what comes after," is a logical process in which propositions are derived from the observation of facts, or in which principles are established from generalizations based on facts. Thus, *a posteriori* reasoning, also called "inductive reasoning," is based initially on experience. (See A PRIORI.)

apparatus criticus
ah-pah-RAH-tuus KRIH-tih-kuus
critical matter

This modern Latin expression, sometimes written **criticus apparatus**, is used to designate supplementary scholarly information, such as variant readings or notes, intended to assist the serious reader of a text. Often abbreviated **apparatus**, explanatory information of this type can have such great bulk that the original text is dwarfed by it, to the delight of the editor and the dismay of the less than devoted reader. "The Yale Edition of Samuel Johnson's works is noted for the completeness of its *apparatus criticus*."

a priori
ah pree-OH-ree
from what is already known

Reasoning *a priori*, literally "from what comes before," is a logical process in which consequences are deduced from principles that are assumed. Thus, *a priori* reasoning, also called "deductive reasoning," is based initially on assumptions that derive from prior knowledge. (See A POSTERIORI.)

aqua et igni interdictus
AH-kwah et IH-gnee in-tehr-DIK-tuus
banished

This expression may be translated as "forbidden water and fire." Caesar and Cicero used **interdicere alicui** (in-tehr-DIH-keh-reh AH-lih-kwee, "to deny to someone") **aqua et igni**, as an expression meaning "to banish." A banished person is denied society; that is, no member of the community may provide him with life's necessities.

aqua pura
AH-kwah POO-rah
distilled water

Literally "pure water."

aqua vitae
AH-kwah WEE-tī
whiskey

Literally "water of life," *aqua vitae*, originally an alchemist's term, appears to be the most amusing euphemism ever invented for hard liquor. Yet no one would deny that *aqua vitae* at times is literally just what its name promises. Physicians are said to carry spirits in their bags, ready for use as restoratives, and formidable amounts of strong drink have been used in Hollywood movies to anesthetize patients about to undergo emergency surgery. The Scandinavians, perhaps because of their long, hard winters, may have been even more justified than the Romans in calling spirits *aqua vitae*. They came up with *akvavit*, a gin-like liquor flavored with caraway seeds, and the alternative spelling of *akvavit* is *aquavit*. But an additional word must be said of the origin of the word *whiskey*: It derives ultimately from the Irish and Scottish Gaelic *uisage beatha*, and what does this phrase mean? "Water of life."

a quo
ah kwoh
from which

arbiter bibendi
AHR-bih-tehr bih-BEN-dee
a toastmaster

Literally "the judge of the drinking," an *arbiter bibendi* in Roman times was much more than a mere toastmaster, as we know the latter term today. Whereas the principal duty of a toastmaster is to preside at a banquet, introducing after-dinner speakers and those who propose toasts, the *arbiter bibendi* kept an eye on the amount of wine drunk at feasts, giving special attention to the proportion of water added to the wine to bring it down to a reasonable strength. In classical times, only the dissolute drank wine at full strength.

arbiter elegantiae
AHR-bih-tehr eh-leh-GAHN-tee-ī
an authority in matters of taste

Anyone established as *arbiter elegantiae* or **arbiter elegantiarum** (eh-leh-GAHN-tee-AH-ruum) is considered the last word in matters of elegance or style.

Arcades ambo
AHR-kah-days AHM-boh
two of a kind

Virgil, in his *Eclogues*, wrote of *Arcades ambo*, literally "Arcadians both," two men of exceptional skill in pastoral poetry and music. Ancient Arcadia, in the Peloponnesus, was perceived as a region of rustic simplicity and contentment, where poetry and music flourished. Thus, in one sense, *Arcades ambo* may be taken as "two persons having like tastes, characteristics, or professions." But the expression has another interpretation: In *Don Juan*, Lord Byron used the phrase ironically: "*Arcades ambo*, *id est* [ihd est]—blackguards both." Byron's intention has overtaken Virgil's, so *Arcades ambo* today more often is used pejoratively.

arcanum arcanorum
ahr-KAH-nuum ahr-kah-NOH-ruum
secret of secrets

The ultimate secret, the secret of nature that supposedly underlies the work of the alchemist, astrologer, and magician.

argumentum
ahr-goo-MEN-tuum
an argument or proof or appeal

Rhetoric was important to the Romans, so they had many phrases in which *argumentum* was combined with other terms, as can be seen by reading on below. It must be made clear here that *argumentum* is not a disagreement, but a proof, especially one adduced to illuminate or clarify.

argumentum ab auctoritate
ahr-goo-MEN-tuum ahb ow-ktoh-rih-TAH-teh
a proof derived from authority

argumentum ab inconvenienti
ahr-goo-MEN-tuum ahb in-kawn-WEH-nee-EN-tee
an appeal based on the hardship or inconvenience involved

argumentum ad absurdum
ahr-goo-MEN-tuum ahd ahb-SUUR-duum
an appeal pointing out the absurdity of one's opponent's point of view, rather than establishing the merits of one's own position

See REDUCTIO AD ABSURDUM.

argumentum ad captandum
ahr-goo-MEN-tuum ahd kah-PTAHN-duum
an appeal based primarily on arousing popular passions

See AD CAPTANDUM VULGUS.

argumentum ad crumenam
ahr-goo-MEN-tuum ahd kroo-MAY-nahm
an appeal based on money or the promise of profit

A **crumena** (kroo-MAY-nah), a leather pouch that held money, was secured by a strap around a Roman's neck. Thus the meaning of *argumentum ad crumenam* as an appeal to the pocketbook—and what is more convincing?

argumentum ad hominem
ahr-goo-MEN-tuum ahd HAW-mih-nem
an argument against the man

Argumentum ad hominem is an effective rhetorical tactic, appealing to feelings rather than intellect, or directed against an opponent's character rather than the subject under discussion. *Argumentum ad hominem* is considered a logical fallacy, in that such an argument fails to prove a point by failing to address it. There is no doubt, however, that in practical politics and in many a court of law, *argumentum ad hominem* is persuasive. (See AD REM and ARGUMENTUM AD REM.)

argumentum ad invidiam
ahr-goo-MEN-tuum ahd ihn-WIH-dee-ahm
an appeal to envy or other undesirable human traits

A powerful tool for the demagogue.

argumentum ad rem
ahr-goo-MEN-tuum ahd rem
a relevant argument

See AD REM.

argumentum baculinum

ahr-goo-MEN-tuum bah-koo-LEE-nuum

an appeal to force

Argumentum baculinum has long been a popular and effective form of persuasion. In *Argumentum baculinum*, the force is suggested by wielding a walking stick (**baculum**), but a *baculum* was also the scepter that symbolized magisterial authority, so the force implied may also be that of governmental authority or legal compulsion.

arma virumque cano

AHR-mah wih-RUUM-kweh KAH-noh

arms and the man I sing

The opening words of Virgil's great epic poem, the *Aeneid*. In an epic, a hero has many demanding adventures, which the poet describes in elevated style. The *Aeneid* traces the experiences of Aeneas, defender of Troy, after the destruction of Troy, in the legendary war precipitated by Helen's abduction by Paris in about 1200 B.C.

arrectis auribus

ah-REH-ktees OW-rih-buus

on the alert

Literally "with ears pricked up." While the phrase describes the characteristic appearance of an animal intent on finding or fighting its prey, it can be used in giving advice to our friends: "In the city, ever *arrectis auribus*."

ars amandi

ahrs ah-MAHN-dee

art of love

Literally "the art of loving."

Ars Amatoria
ahrs ah-mah-TOH-ree-ah
The Art of Love

The title of Ovid's work on the amatory art, with full accounts of how to find and keep a lover. This how-to book of ancient Rome—it was published about 2 B.C.—is still worth reading. Within a few years after *Ars Amatoria* appeared, Ovid was banished from Rome by Emperor Augustus, and he died an exile in A.D. 17. Ovid, in his autobiographical work *Tristia*, gives two reasons for his exile: *carmen*, "song," and *error*, an unspecified "indiscretion." From his extended justifications in *Tristia* and other late works, it is clear that Ovid believed *Ars Amatoria* had offended the prudish Augustus.

ars artium
ahrs AHR-tee-uum
logic

Literally "the art of arts."

ars est celare artem
ahrs est keh-LAH-reh AHR-tem
true art conceals the means by which it is achieved

Ovid's maxim in *Ars Amatoria*, literally "it is art to conceal art," has it that in the best works of art the audience is not distracted by the artist's technique, but responds instead to the power of the work, as the artist intended. True art must appear artless. *Ars est celare artem* as a critical evaluation of a work of art, thus, is a high compliment.

ars gratia artis
ahrs GRAH-tee-ah AHR-tis
art for art's sake

The motto of the true artist, now preempted by Hollywood: Metro-Goldwyn-Mayer, the motion picture producers, use it as part of the M-G-M trademark.

ars longa, vita brevis
ahrs LAWN-gah WEE-tah BREH-wihs
art is long, but life is short

The Greek physician Hippocrates coined this aphorism, here given in its Latin translation, telling us that the art of healing has a life much longer than that of its practitioner (and patient, we might add), but *ars longa, vita brevis* is generally extended to all the arts today. The principal intent, no matter how *ars* is interpreted, is to point out that we are mortal and must anticipate death. Longfellow, in his "Psalm of Life," put it this way for all of us:

> Art is long, and Time is fleeting,
> And our hearts, though stout and brave,
> Still, like muffled drums, are beating
> Funeral marches to the grave.

A sobering thought.

ars moriendi
ahrs maw-ree-EN-dee
the art of dying

The Romans put much store in dying nobly. (See PAETE, NON DOLET.)

ars poetica
ahrs paw-AY-tih-kah
the art of poetry

Also the title, *Ars Poetica*, of an epistolary poem of Horace, written about 20 B.C., expounding his literary theory.

arte perire sua
AHR-teh peh-REE-reh SOO-ah
to trip oneself up

Here—recall the English adjective "artful," as in the Artful
Dodger in *Oliver Twist*—ars takes on a meaning akin to wiles
or cunning or machinations, so a literal translation of *arte perire
sua* is "to perish by one's own machinations." The expression is
not unlike our own "hoist with his own petard," literally "blown
up by his own bomb," but understood as "trapped by his own
machinations."

artes perditae
AHR-tays PEHR-dih-tī
lost arts

Any skills forgotten by a culture are *artes perditae*. "Addition
and multiplication, as a trip to any supermarket will demonstrate, are *artes perditae*."

artes, scientia, veritas
AHR-tays skee-EN-tee-ah WEH-rih-tahs
arts, science, truth

Motto of the University of Michigan.

Artium Baccalaureus
AHR-tee-uum bah-kah-LOW-ray-uus
Bachelor of Arts

Abbreviated **A.B.** or **B.A.** This, of course, is the undergradu-
ate degree awarded by colleges and universities. The derivation
of the term is not clear. It has been suggested that the medieval
Latin term *baccalaureus*, "bachelor," was adapted from **bac-
calarius** (bah-kah-LOW-ree-uus), meaning "laborer" or "ten-
ant." This discussion is intended solely to suggest the possibly

humble origin of the bachelor of arts degree, awarded formally after four years' hard labor or, too often, after four years' tenancy in a college dormitory.

Artium Magister
AHR-tee-uum mah-GIS-tehr
Master of Arts

Abbreviated **A.M.** or **M.A.** Another university degree.

asinus asinum fricat
AH-sih-nuus AH-sih-nuum FRIH-kaht
one fool rubs the other's back

Two people who lavish excessive praise on one another—perhaps no one else sees anything praiseworthy in either of them—exemplify *asinus asinum fricat*, literally "the ass rubs the ass." No group has a corner on the market for *asinus asinum fricat*. Wherever people of small talent gather, someone sooner or later will establish a chapter of the Mutual Admiration Society.

a tergo
ah TEHR-goh
from behind

This expression is applied most often today to a position in sexual intercourse in which the male lies behind the female.

auctor ignotus
OW-ktawr ih-GNOH-tuus
an unknown author

Not a putdown. An *auctor ignotus* is an author whose work has not gained the recognition it merits.

audaces fortuna iuvat (or juvat)
ow-DAH-kays fawr-TOO-nah YOO-waht
fortune favors the bold

Also given as **audentes** (ow-DEN-tays, "the daring") **fortuna iuvat**. This motto for the bold and successful and for those who aspire to success was cited by many Roman writers. The English proverb "Nothing ventured, nothing gained" captures the spirit of this common Roman saying.

audemus iura (or jura) nostra defendere
ow-DAY-muus YOO-rah NAW-strah deh-FEN-deh-reh
we dare defend our rights

The motto of Alabama, perhaps calling attention to that state's dedication to protecting its rights against infringement by the federal government.

audi alteram partem
OW-dee AHL-teh-rahm PAHR-tem
there are two sides to every question

Literally "hear the other side." A plea for reason and fairness in discussion.

aura popularis
OW-rah paw-puu-LAH-rihs
temporary celebrity

Cicero's expression for the public's favorite at a particular time, who is said to be enjoying *aura popularis*, literally "the popular breeze." But breezes subside.

aurea mediocritas
OW-ray-ah meh-dee-AW-krih-tahs
moderation in all things

Those of us who are satisfied with lives of security and contentment seek *aurea mediocritas*, literally "the golden mean." We are willing to live out our days without taking great risks, without indulging in excesses. *Aurea mediocritas* is an expression used by Horace, in his *Odes*; he intended it in the meaning just described: "Who loves the golden mean is safe from the poverty of a hovel and free from the envy of a palace."

aureo hamo piscari
OW-ray-oh HAH-moh pih-SKAH-ree
money talks

Literally "to fish with a golden hook," *aureo hamo piscari* recognizes the marvelous persuasiveness of cash on the barrelhead. This in not unlike **auro quaeque ianua panditur** (OW-roh KWĪ-kweh YAH-noo-ah PAHN-dih-tuur), which we know as "a golden key opens any door," but which translates literally as "any door is opened by means of gold."

auri sacra fames
OW-ree SAH-krah FAH-mays
money-mad

Those who live only to acquire wealth are characterized by Virgil as having *auri sacra fames*, literally "the cursed hunger for gold."

Aurora
ow-ROH-rah
goddess of the morning

In Roman mythology, Aurora was responsible for such duties as extinguishing stars at the end of night. But there was more to her: She had a weakness for mortal men, her favorite being Tithonus, son of the king of Troy. After stealing him away, she inveigled Jupiter into giving Tithonus immortality, but neglected to arrange for eternal youth for the poor fellow. In time, he grew old and unappealing, so Aurora locked him in his room. All that was heard from Tithonus from then on was a feeble cry from time to time. As a final act of mercy, Aurora turned him into a grasshopper. We know Aurora today mostly in the terms *aurora australis* and *aurora borealis*, the southern lights and northern lights, which delight and mystify us, pronounced in English ə-ROH-rə aw-STRAY-ləs and boh-ree-AL-əs.

auspicium melioris aevi
ow-SPIH-kee-uum meh-lee-OH-ris Ī-wee
an omen of a better time

Yet another expression revealing the Romans' deep concern with auguries. Finding a white stone, a flower growing in a rock, or any other sign of good things to come—*auspicium melioris aevi*—was taken quite seriously.

Austriae est imperare orbi universo
OW-stree-ī est im-peh-RAH-reh AWR-bee
OO-nih-WEHR-soh
it is Austria's destiny to rule the world

The motto of Emperor Frederick III, one of the Hapsburgs. The fact that the Hapsburgs no longer dictate to anybody, not even the Austrians, is a commentary on the impermanence of power. The abbreviation of Frederick's motto, whether rendered in German or in Latin, is itself worthy of mention: **A.E.I.O.U.** is the abbreviation of the German *Alles Erdreich ist Oesterreich unterthan*, "the whole world is subjected to Austria," retaining for moderns the irony as well as the initial letters of the Latin phrase.

aut bibat aut abeat
owt BIH-baht owt AHB-ay-aht
you're either for us or against us

This saying, a borrowing from the Greek, in the literal sense is taken as "let him either drink or depart." In an extended meaning, *aut bibat aut abeat* can be used to force participation on an unwilling member of a plan or conspiracy. Either the hesitating fellow goes along with the others, or he is no longer welcome.

aut Caesar aut nihil
owt KĪ-sahr owt NIH-hil
all or nothing

Literally "either Caesar (that is, emperor of Rome) or nothing," associated with Julius Caesar, who said he would sooner be number one man in a village than number two in Rome, and a motto of Cesare Borgia (1476–1507). The favorite son of Pope Alexander VI, Borgia was known for his crimes and violence, even against members of his own family. One of his lovable practices, according to legend, was that of poisoning the wine of rivals before joining them in toasting mutual friendship. Borgia's failure to achieve his ambition to seize total power reflects badly on the efficacy of his underhanded methods. *Aut Caesar aut nihil* is also given as **aut Caesar aut nullus** (NUU-luus, "nobody"), with the same meaning.

aut disce aut discede
OWT DIH-skeh owt dih-SKAY-deh
either learn or leave

A suitable motto for a school sufficiently principled, not to mention well endowed, to be able to insist on excellent academic standards.

aut viam inveniam aut faciam
owt WEE-ahm in-WEH-nee-ahm owt FAH-kee-ahm
where there's a will there's a way

Literally "I'll either find a way or make one," *aut viam inveniam aut faciam* is the credo of the person who plugs along, unwilling ever to admit defeat. Such a person is determined, not obstinate.

aut vincere aut mori
owt WIN-keh-reh owt MAW-ree
victory or death

A Roman motto, literally "either to conquer or to die," intended to inspire soldiers preparing for battle, also found (in French) in a stanza of the *Marseillaise*. Gilbert and Sullivan mock this spirit in their *Pirates of Penzance*. The fair young maidens exhort the departing constabulary to fight bravely against the threatening pirates: "Go, ye heroes, go and die." Anyone who has ever prepared for battle will understand the effectiveness of such encouragement.

ave atque vale
AH-weh AHT-kweh WAH-lay
hail and farewell

Ave, "hail," was the Roman equivalent of "hello," and *vale* the equivalent of "goodbye," as well as the Roman farewell to the dead. Catullus used this expression in closing a poem on the death of his brother: "Atque in perpetuum, frater (in per-PEH-too-uum FRAH-ter), ave atque vale." "And forever, brother, hail and farewell!"

ave Caesar, morituri te salutant
AH-weh KĪ-sahr MAW-rih-TOO-ree tay sah-LOO-tahnt
hail, Caesar, those who are about to die salute you

A line suitable for the clever schoolboy making his appearance before a board of examiners. The words are those of Roman gladiators entering the arena to launch into mortal combat. Suetonius tells us in his *Lives of the Caesars* that Emperor Claudius (A.D. 41–54) so enjoyed these spectacles, he ordered that even those who fell accidentally be put to death. He wanted to watch their faces as they died. No wonder the gladiators referred to themselves as "those who are about to die." The full expression is also given as **ave, Caesar, morituri te salutamus** (sah-loo-TAH-mus), "hail, Caesar, we who are about to die salute you."

ave Maria
AH-weh mah-REE-ah
hail Mary

The angels' salutation to the Virgin, from Luke, in English pronounced AH-vay mah-REE-ə.

a verbis ad verbera
ah WEHR-bees ahd WEHR-beh-rah
from words to blows

An expression useful in describing a discussion that is heating up.

Ave Regina Caelorum
AH-weh ray-GEE-nah kī-LOH-ruum
Hail, Queen of Heaven

Title of a hymn in honor of the Virgin, the Queen of Heaven.

a vinculo matrimonii
ah WIN-kuu-loh mah-trih-MOH-nee-ee
an absolute divorce

A divorce *a vinculo matrimonii*, literally "from the bond of marriage," and also called a divorce *a vinculo*, is one that releases husband and wife from all legal commitments of marriage. It is interesting to note that *vinculum* (WIN-kuu-luum, "bond") also means "noose" and "chain."

beatae memoriae
bay-AH-tī meh-MAW-ree-ī
of blessed memory

Used on tombstones and memorial plaques.

Beata Maria
bay-AH-tah mah-REE-ah
Blessed Mary

Maria, of course, is the Virgin Mary. Other Latin expressions are also used in referring to Mary, including **Beata Virgo** (WEER-goh, Blessed Virgin) and **Beata Virgo Maria** (Blessed Virgin Mary). The abbreviations **B.M.** and **B.V.** for *Beata Maria* and *Beata Virgo* are sometimes seen.

beati pacifici
bay-AH-tee pah-KIH-fih-kee
blessed are the peacemakers

In Matthew, the opening words of the eighth beatitude of the Sermon on the Mount, concluding "for they shall be called sons of God."

beati pauperes spiritu
beh-AH-tee POW-peh-rehs SPIH-rih-too
blessed are the poor in spirit

In Matthew, the opening words of the Sermon on the Mount, concluding "for theirs is the kingdom of heaven." The irrepressible Alexander Pope wrote a beatitude of his own: "Blessed is the man who expects nothing, for he shall never be disappointed."

beati possidentes
beh-AH-tee PAW-sih-DEN-tays
possession is nine points of the law

Literally "blessed are those who possess" (for they shall receive). This expression finds its principal meaning in conveying the idea that one may claim property most easily before the law when one has physical possession of it—consider the longtime squatter on land deeded to another person. In a cynical vein, *beati possidentes*, translated literally, may be taken as a commentary on the uncanny knack of the haves to acquire ever more, while the have-nots acquire ever less.

beatus
beh-AH-tuus
the blessed person

See ADVOCATUS DIABOLI.

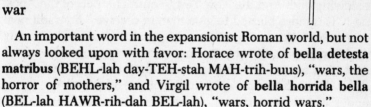

bellum
BEHL-luum
war

An important word in the expansionist Roman world, but not always looked upon with favor: Horace wrote of **bella detesta matribus** (BEHL-lah day-TEH-stah MAH-trih-buus), "wars, the horror of mothers," and Virgil wrote of **bella horrida bella** (BEL-lah HAWR-rih-dah BEL-lah), "wars, horrid wars."

bene
BEH-neh
well

A noteworthy observation incorporating this adverb is **bene qui latuit** (kwee LAH-too-iht) **bene vixit** (WEE-ksiht), literally "he who has lived in obscurity has lived well." The line is from

Tristia, Ovid's extended lament about his enforced exile from Rome, and its meaning is not to be taken as a panegyric for the simple life. Rather, Ovid is expressing bitterness over the way things have turned out for him, telling us that the powerful— Emperor Augustus *et al.*—are envious of brilliance and attractiveness in others, so *bene qui latuit bene vixit*, "keep a low profile if you wish to survive." Whistle-blowers, beware.

beneficium accipere libertatem est vendere
beh-neh-FIH-kee-uum ahk-KIHP-eh-reh
lee-behr-TAH-tem est WEHN-deh-reh
to accept a favor is to sell one's freedom

In *Hamlet*, Polonius advises his son:

> Neither a borrower, nor a lender be;
> For loan oft loses both itself and friend,
> And borrowing dulls the edge of husbandry.

So much for Shakespeare's wisdom on extending kindness as well as receiving it. Let's turn to a Roman playwright. *Beneficium accipere libertatem est vendere*, a maxim attributed to Publilius Syrus, recognizes only the problems of those on the receiving end. And the New Testament? The Acts of the Apostles: "It is more blessed to give than to receive." So traditional sources of wisdom appear to agree that acts of kindness may lead to misery rather than to improvement in the quality of our lives, and we are left confused and uncertain. Perhaps everything depends on the spirit in which we give and the terms under which we borrow.

bis dat qui cito dat
bihs daht kwee KIH-toh daht
he gives twice who quickly gives

This Latin proverb, quoted by Cervantes in *Don Quixote*, may serve as a fitting motto for professional fund-raisers, who so often have to badger self-professed donors into delivering on their pledges. There is little joy in such gifts, nor is there satis-

faction in any act of charity or kindness given reluctantly and
only after repeated appeals.

bis repetita placent
bihs reh-peh-TEE-tah PLAH-kent
a little originality, please

A derogatory comment, literally "the things that please are
those that are asked for again and again," appropriate for a
derivative work. Horace was telling us in *bis repetita placent*
that certain works of art please once, but others, tried and true,
are imitated widely and always please. Thus, when we see a
work obviously patterned after a previous, successful work, we
may say *bis repetita placent* or merely *bis repetita*, telling the
creator of the imitative work that he is catering to the public's
taste rather than attempting something original.

bis vivit qui bene vivit
bihs WEE-wiht kwee BEH-neh WEE-wiht
he lives twice who lives well

Milton, in *Paradise Lost*, couched the same wisdom in these
words:

> Nor love thy life, nor hate; but what thou liv'st
> Live well; how long or short permit to Heaven.

So we are being told that quality of life is much more important
than longevity. But *bis vivit qui bene vivit*, besides counseling
us to lead productive lives, offers a consoling thought to recall
when a friend dies young.

bona fide
BAW-nah FIH-deh
in good faith

This phrase can also be translated as "honestly," "sincerely,"
or any other word or expression denoting "without deception."

Bona fide has been used as an adjective phrase in our own language so often that we all know it by its English pronunciation, BOH-nə-fīd. To produce *bona fides* (English pronunciation BOH-nə FĪ-deez) means to show good intentions in dealing with others, show credentials, prove one's identity or ability, etc. No fraud or deceit is intended or shown. (See MALA FIDE.)

bonis avibus
BAW-nees AH-wih-buus
under favorable signs

Literally "under good birds," a phrase indicating that the omens are favorable for a contemplated action. The Romans relied so heavily on birds, **aves** (AH-ways), as tools in divination that the noun **avis** (AH-wihs) is translated as "sign" or "omen" as well as "bird," and **avi mala** (MAH-lah) and **avi sinistra** (sih-NIH-strah) mean "bad omens." But the Romans were not the only ones who found magic in birds. Consider, for example, the persistent use of the dove as a symbol of peace, innocence, and love.

bonum vinum laetificat cor hominis
BAW-nuum WEE-nuum lī-TIH-fih-kaht kawr
HAW-mih-nihs
good wine gladdens a person's heart

The Psalms speak of "wine that maketh glad the heart of man," referring to the bountiful favors provided by God. In the modern world, *bonum vinum laetificat* may find wider application as a slogan for promoting consumption of wine and spirits.

brutum fulmen
BROO-tuum FUUL-men
an empty threat

Brutum fulmen, literally "an insensible thunderbolt," reminds us of Pliny's phrase **bruta fulmina et vana** (BROO-tah FUUL-mih-nah et WAH-nah), "thunderbolts that strike blindly and in vain." Those who argue bombastically or who threaten idly without the inclination or ability to follow up on their threats are said to offer only *brutum fulmen*. One can also apply the phrase to governments that continually threaten their adversaries but never make good on the threats—to the relief of the rest of us, whose sons would be the ones sent to fulfill the threats.

c or ca.

See CIRCA.

cacoëthes carpendi
kah-koh-AY-thehs kahr-PEN-dee
a mania for finding fault

Cacoëthes, derived from *kakoethes*, a Greek word that combines *kakos*, "bad," with *ethos*, "habit," describes any compulsion or uncontrollable urge. *Cacoëthes* can be used alone to mean "mania" or "passion," even "disease." With *carpendi*, a form of *carpere* (KAHR-peh-reh), meaning "to pluck," as fruit from a tree, the phrase becomes highly useful in describing the uncontrollable urge of an inveterate nitpicker.

cacoëthes loquendi
kah-koh-AY-thehs loh-KWEN-dee
compulsive talking

Anyone who goes on talking and talking and talking and talking may be said to exhibit *cacoëthes loquendi*. (See CACOËTHES CARPENDI.)

cacoëthes scribendi
kah-koh-AY-thehs skree-BEN-dee
an incurable itch to write

Another form of *cacoëthes*. In the fuller phrase **insanabile** (in-sah-NAH-bih-lay, "incurable") **cacoëthes scribendi**, Juvenal in his *Satires* harshly described the compulsion to write—that is, to become a published writer—still prevalent today. We see the phrase used now as an uncharitable appraisal of a writer deemed untalented, implicitly advising said person to abandon writing and pursue some more suitable vocation. Juvenal's full statement is worthy of translation: "An inveterate and incurable itch for writing besets many and grows old in their sick hearts." No laughing matter is this incurable itch.

cadit quaestio
KAH-dit KWI-stee-oh
the argument collapses

Cadit quaestio, literally translated as "the question falls," is said when the central idea of an argument or a legal case collapses: "*Cadit quaestio*, there is nothing further to be said; let us move on to other matters."

caeca invidia est
KĪ-kah in-WIH-dee-ah est
envy is blind

We are accustomed to thinking of love as blind, but Livy's aphorism *caeca invidia est* tells us that envy also is blind: Those possessed by envy overlook facts that would alleviate or eliminate the debilitating condition.

caeli enarrant gloriam Dei
KĪ-lee eh-NAHR-rahnt GLOH-ree-ahm DEH-ee
the heavens bespeak the glory of God

Often abbreviated *caeli enarrant*, this quotation from the Psalms cites the stars and the planets as brilliant evidence of the wisdom and power of God. *Caeli enarrant* is a fitting expression on seeing the full moon or a particularly spectacular celestial display. *Caeli enarrant* is also a fitting comment—a star is born

—on the brilliant debut of a musical prodigy, an outstanding new writer or actor, or any young person coming to the favorable attention of the public for the first time.

caelum non animum ...

See COELUM NON ANIMUM ...

caetera desunt
KĪ-tay-rah DAY-suunt
the rest are missing

See CETERA DESUNT.

caeteris paribus
KĪ-teh-rees PAH-rih-buus
other things being equal

Also given as **ceteris** (KAY-teh-rees) **paribus**. "The President said that *caeteris paribus* he would appoint a woman to the post."

Campus Martius
KAHM-puus MAHR-tee-uus
the field of Mars

In the early republic, Romans used the term *Campus Martius* to designate a field on the eastern bank of the Tiber that they used as an encampment when the army was mobilized—Mars, of course, was the Roman god of war. The *Campus Martius* was also used for athletic contests, in themselves a kind of warfare, and for meetings of the **comitia** (koh-MEE-tee-ah), the assembly of the Roman people for the election of consuls, magistrates, and other officials, as well as to decide on mobilization of the army.

caput mortuum
KAH-puut MOR-too-uum
worthless residue

The literal meaning of *caput mortuum* is "death's head," a skull. The term was used by the alchemists to designate the residue in a flask after distillation was complete. *Caput mortuum* now can be taken as any worthless residue, even a useless person.

caput mundi
KAH-puut MUUN-dee
the Big Apple

The Romans thought of Rome as *caput mundi*, literally "the head—the capital—of the world," and perhaps justifiably so. After all, Poe spoke of "the glory that was Greece and the grandeur that was Rome." And did not all roads lead to Rome? Those who boost their own hometowns may use *caput mundi* in the same way the Romans did.

caritas
KAH-rih-tahs
love, charity

Forgetting that charity designates "love of humanity," we tend to think of it exclusively as "giving to the poor." By *caritas* the Romans meant "dearness" or "high price." (**Carus** [KAH-ruus], meaning "dear," is an etymological ancestor of the word "whore.") Thus, when Cicero wrote of a year in which the cost of living was high, he used the phrase **annonae** (AHN-noh-nī, "crops") **caritas**. Eventually *caritas* designated another kind of dearness, the highest love or fellowship—charity as we now know it in the sense conveyed in Corinthians: "And now abideth faith, hope, charity, these three; but the greatest of these is charity."

carpe diem
KAHR-peh DEE-em

enjoy, enjoy

This famous advice, literally "seize the day," is from Horace's *Odes*. The full thought is **carpe diem, quam minimum credula postero** (kwahm MIH-nih-muum KRAY-duu-lah PAW-ster-oh), which may be translated as "enjoy today, trusting little in tomorrow." Thus, *carpe diem* from ancient times until the present has been advice often and variously expressed: Enjoy yourself while you have the chance; eat, drink, and be merry, for tomorrow we die; make hay while the sun shines; enjoy yourself, it's later than you think. In another century *carpe diem* was also an exhortation to maidens to give up their virginity and enjoy all the pleasures of life.

Robert Herrick (1591–1674):

> Gather ye rosebuds while ye may,
> Old Time is still a-flying,
> And this same flower that smiles today
> Tomorrow will be dying.

castigat ridendo mores
KAH-stih-gaht ree-DEN-doh MOH-rays

laughter succeeds where lecturing won't

The literal translation of *castigat ridendo mores* is "it (or he or she) corrects customs (or manners) by laughing at them." This phrase, therefore, gives us the essence of satire, whose target is the folly of mankind, and whose technique is ridicule.

casus belli
KAH-suus BEL-lee

justification for making war

Casus literally means a "fall" or "falling," but the word was used by the Romans in many ways, signifying an occasion, opportunity, misfortune, mishap, destruction, downfall, etc. Thus, Virgil refers to **casus urbis Troianae** (UUR-bis troy-AH-nī), "the fall of the city of Troy." *Belli* is the genitive of **bellum** (BEL-luum, "war"), and Cicero refers to **bellum domesticum** (doh-MEH-stih-kuum), "familial strife," telling us that, alas, marital problems and family disputes are not a recent invention. Historians seek to establish the *casus belli* for each of the many wars that have befallen mankind. Diplomats, we expect, are concerned with avoiding a *casus belli* when relations between nations are strained. But those intent on making war are sure to find a *casus belli* or invent one.

casus foederis
KAH-suus FOY-deh-ris
a situation triggering action under a treaty

Casus in its many meanings is discussed under CASUS BELLI. *Foederis* is the genitive of **foedus** (FOY-duus), which literally is "a league" or "an alliance between two states," but came to mean the document creating the alliance. Those of us who have studied the events leading up to World War I may recall that intricate networks of alliances had been set up among the nations of Europe. When an attack was made on one of the nations so allied, it became the *casus foederis*, obliging all the other nations in one way or another to commit their resources to the tragic war that followed. *Foedus* is not restricted in meaning to alliances between nations. Cicero spoke of **foedus amorum** (ah-MOH-ruum), "a love pact," surely a happier and more narrowly intended agreement.

causa sine qua non
KOW-sah SIH-neh kwah nohn
a necessary condition

Causa sine qua non is literally "a cause without which not," so we can readily understand the meaning of the phrase. *Causa* occurs in other phrases as well: **causa causans** (KOW-sahns) can be translated as "an initiating cause," and **causa causata** (kow-SAH-tah) as "a cause owing its existence to a *causa causans* or, perhaps, to another *causa causata*," thus giving us a way to use Latin in arguing the eternal question of who did what to whom first. Theologians use these terms in describing God and His works, God being *causa causans*, and creation *causa causata*.

caveant consules ne quid detrimenti respublica capiat
KAH-way-ahnt KAWN-suu-lays nay kwid
day-tree-MEN-tee rays-POO-blih-kah KAH-pee-aht
beware, consuls, that the republic is not harmed

Usually abbreviated *caveant consules*, "consuls beware," this elegant sentence was the formula used by the Roman Senate to invite the consuls—the two chief magistrates of the republic—to designate a dictator in times of crisis. Presumably there was no time available for the ordinary processes of government, involving time-consuming debate. In modern use, this formula becomes ominous, alerting a legally constituted government to the threat of replacement by a dictatorship if the people's dissatisfaction with that government is not recognized and reversed.

caveat emptor
KAH-way-aht EMP-tawr
let the buyer beware

The rule of law warning potential purchasers of goods or services that they are not protected during a transaction against failure of the sellers to live up to the bargain except to the extent that the sales contract stipulates. By this rule, the purchaser, not the seller, is responsible for protecting the purchaser in the transaction. *Caveat emptor* is the opposite of **caveat venditor** (WEN-dih-tawr). Whereas *caveat emptor* has a long history in common law, *caveat venditor* is just now coming into prominence as a result of the consumer rights movement. Under *caveat venditor*, the seller is assumed to be more sophisticated than the purchaser and so must bear responsibility for protecting the unwary purchaser. The purchaser, *emptor*, is a child who must be protected against his own mistakes, while the seller, *venditor*, is the big, bad wolf lying in wait for Little Red Riding Hood. So while the two rules struggle for preeminence, attorneys gleefully watch—and litigate.

cave canem
KAH-weh KAH-nem
beware of the dog

This friendly warning, commonly inscribed on doors of Roman homes, was found on the door of a house in Pompeii during excavation of that ancient city, rediscovered in 1748. Pompeii had been buried during an eruption of Mount Vesuvius in A.D. 79. Finding a homely reminder of the day-to-day lives of an ancient people whose lives were snuffed out suddenly by catastrophe reinforces the validity of the warning found on old clocks: ULTIMA FORSAN (UUL-tih-mah FAWR-sahn), "perhaps the last hour." The inhabitants of Pompeii had little warning their time had come. How many of them had followed the injunction CARPE DIEM?

cave quid dicis, quando, et cui
KAH-weh kwid DEE-kis, KWAHN-doh, et KOO-ee
beware what you say, when, and to whom

Excellent advice for all of us. (See VIR SAPIT QUI PAUCA LOQUITUR.)

cedant arma togae
KAY-dahnt AHR-mah TOH-gī
military power must be subordinate to civil authority

The motto of Wyoming, literally "let arms yield to the gown." Cicero, discussing in *De Officiis* his term as consul, used these words to affirm the primacy of civil authority under his rule, giving us a maxim we may cite to warn against military dictatorship. *Arma*, "arms," represents the military; *toga* (TOH-gah), the garment worn by Roman citizens in their peacetime lives, represents civil authority. (See TOGA.)

certiorari
KEHR-tee-oh-RAH-ree
to be made certain

A writ of *certiorari*, in English pronounced sur-shee-ə-RAIR-ee, is a legal document calling for delivery to a higher court of the record of a proceeding before a lower court. The purpose of calling for the record is to enable judicial review of the action taken by the lower court. The basis for issuing the writ is a complaint that an injustice has been done by the lower court.

certum est quia impossibile est
KEHR-tuum est KWEE-ah im-paw-SIH-bih-leh est
it is certain because it is impossible

A maxim of Tertullian (third century A.D.), in *De Carne Christi*, warning us that in matters of faith we are not to believe the evidence presented to us by our eyes and ears. In light of our limited understanding as mere mortals, the apparent impossibility of the truth of the supernatural is an argument for acceptance, rather than for rejection, of the supernatural.

cessante causa cessat et effectus
keh-SAHN-tay KOW-sah KEH-saht et ef-FEK-tuus
when the cause is removed, the effect disappears

The validity of *cessante causa cessat et effectus*, literally "the cause ceasing, the effect also ceases," is demonstrable in most of life's activities, but not in human behavior, if we are to believe the psychoanalyst. For example, while pain caused by an aching tooth may disappear once the tooth is treated, pain suffered in childhood may plague adults all through their lives.

cetera desunt
KAY-teh-rah DAY-suunt
the rest are missing

This scholarly notation (also given as **caetera desunt**) is used to indicate that parts of a work have not been found despite careful research. "The full text of the verse by Sappho has never been found, so the missing portions are marked *cetera desunt*."

ceteris paribus
KAY-teh-rees PAH-rih-buus
other things being equal

See CAETERIS PARIBUS.

cf.

See CONFER.

circa
KIHR-kah
about

This scholar's term, in English pronounced SUR-kə, and abbreviated *c* or *ca*., indicates uncertainty about a date. "It is generally assumed that Chaucer was born *c* A.D. 1340." "The vase was dated *ca*. fourth century B.C."

codex
KOH-deks
a manuscript parchment; a code of laws

Codex, originally spelled **caudex** (KOW-deks), first meant "tree trunk," but eventually acquired additional meanings. For example, Juvenal used *codex* to mean "a wooden block," to which men were tied as punishment. Terence used *codex* as a term of derision, the equivalent of "blockhead." Finally *codex* came to mean a book made of bound wooden slabs, with printing scratched into wax coatings on the slabs. But *codex* also has the meaning of "a code of laws." Two famous **codices**, plural of *codex* and pronounced KOH-dih-kays (in English KOHD-ə-seez), are the **Codex Alexandrinus** (ah-lek-sahn-DREE-nuus) and the **Codex Sinaiticus** (see-NĪ-tih-kuus), but there are many others, including the **Codex Juris Canonici** (YUU-ris kah-NOH-nih-kee), the official collection of ecclesiastical laws of the Roman Catholic Church.

coelum non animum mutant qui trans mare currunt
KOY-luum nohn AH-nih-muum MOO-tahnt kwee
trahns MAH-reh KUUR-ruunt
those who cross the sea change the sky, not their spirits

In this delightful sentence from Horace's *Epistles*, we are cautioned that a change of scene—here *coelum*, "the heavens," also given as **caelum** (KĪ-luum)—does not change us: As we travel from one place to another, what we see with our eyes may change dramatically, but we are the same people we were when we started our journey. If we are to credit Horace, then, we cannot flee our destinies, nor by flight can we change what is fundamental to our nature: The grass is not greener on the other side of the street. Fortunately, in *Paradise Lost* Milton sends a happier message:

> The mind is its own place, and in itself
> Can make a Heav'n of Hell, a Hell of Heav'n.

cogito ergo sum
KOH-gih-toh EHR-goh SUUM
I think, therefore I exist

One of the most famous of all philosophic axioms, known—perhaps imperfectly—by every freshman student of philosophy. Descartes, in his *Discourse on Method*, used it as the starting point for his philosophic system.

coitus interruptus
koh-EE-tuus in-tehr-RUUP-tuus
interrupted coitus

collegium
kawl-LAY-gee-uum
colleagueship

A *collegium*—in Roman times the word described the connection between a pair of colleagues as well as within a group of colleagues—can be applied now to members of any group united by common interest or pursuits: a college faculty or department, a society of scholars, an ecclesiastical group living together to pursue a common purpose, etc.

compos mentis
KAWM-paws MEN-tis
of sound mind

A person in his right mind is adjudged *compos mentis*, translated more literally as "in full possession of mental powers," while a person not of sound mind is said to be **non** (nohn) **compos mentis**. The two terms are used loosely today by people unqualified to make either judgment. More properly the two expressions find use in legal writing and court testimony.

compos sui
KAWM-paws SOO-ee
master of himself

Compos sui is a condition few of us can aspire to in this world of big government and big corporations. Unlike the English poet W. E. Henley (1849–1903), we cannot declaim:

> I am the master of my fate:
> I am the captain of my soul.

conditio sine qua non
kawn-DEE-tee-oh SIH-neh kwah nohn
indispensable condition

When an agreement stands or falls on the inclusion of a particular condition, that condition may be called a *conditio sine qua non*, literally "a condition without which not." (See CAUSA SINE QUA NON.)

confer
KAWN-fehr
compare

The abbreviation of *confer*, **cf.**, is seen in English most often in scholarly writing. The abbreviation may be used, for example, to invite readers to compare an author's discussion with that presented in another work, but the important fact to bear in mind is that *cf.* does not mean merely "see" or "see also." The full Latin word *confer* is never seen in modern texts.

confiteor
kawn-FIH-tay-awr
I confess

The opening word of the Catholic general confession said at the beginning of the mass.

Congregatio de Propaganda Fide
kawn-greh-GAH-tee-oh day praw-pah-GAHN-dah
FIH-deh
Congregation for the Propagation of the Faith

The committee that supervises messages and missions for the Vatican. The committee members are cardinals and other church officials.

coniunctis (or conjunctis) viribus
kawn-YUUNK-tees WEE-rih-buus
with united powers

Anyone acting in concert with others can be said to be acting *conjunctis viribus* toward a common goal. "The Allied Powers pledged to act *conjunctis viribus* when an attack was directed at any of the several nations."

consensus
kawn-SEN-suus
agreement

This word, taken into English with the same meaning as its Latin ancestor, bedevils poor spellers of English, who fail to associate *consensus* with the English word "consent." Thus, we often see the misspelling "concensus," reflecting a confusion with the word "census." The Latin word **census** (KEN-suus) has a meaning somewhat like that of our English "census": The Romans registered all citizens and their property for purposes of taxation, calling the registration a *census*. "Consent," as one already knows, has little to do with taxation. The word "consent" derives from **consentire** (kawn-sen-TIH-reh), "to agree," whose past participle is *consensus*. While it is primarily to help poor spellers that *consensus* is given its own entry here, *consensus*, as soon will be seen, is central—forgive me—to several useful Latin expressions.

consensus audacium
kawn-SEN-suus ow-DAH-kee-uum

a conspiracy

Cicero used this phrase, literally "agreement of rash (men),"
to describe conspiracies by people intent on some nefarious
purpose. In his time, Cicero acted as self-appointed watchdog
of men in government and frequently held forth in the Senate
to accuse his political enemies of conspiracy.

consensus facit legem
kawn-SEN-suus FAH-kit LAY-gem

consent makes law

The principle that an agreement between two parties is bind-
ing if the agreement does not in any way violate existing law.

consensus gentium
kawn-SEN-suus GEN-tee-uum

widespread agreement

This phrase, literally "unanimity of the nations," is used to
describe perfect or nearly perfect agreement on some matter
by everyone concerned. So a generally accepted belief or opin-
ion may be described as a *consensus gentium*.

consensus omnium
kawn-SEN-suus AW-mnee-uum

agreement of all

A happy situation, in which all parties involved in a discussion
of policy, procedure, or the like have reached unanimity. Another form of this phrase is **consensu** (kawn-SEN-soo) **omnium**,
with the meaning "by general consent." "We acted *consensu
omnium* in all decisions affecting our members' welfare." Tacitus, in his *Annales*, made telling use of *consensu omnium* in

describing an inept politician: **Omnium consensu capax imperii nisi imperasset** (KAH-pahks im-PEH-ree-ee NIH-sih im-peh-RAHS-set), "By general consent, he would have been considered capable of governing if he had never governed." A classic putdown.

consilio manuque
kawn-SIH-lee-oh mah-NOO-kweh
by stratagem and manual labor

The motto of Figaro in Beaumarchais's *Barber of Seville*. Figaro was a barber who used wit and resourcefulness in struggling against the abuses of government. *Consilio manuque* could well serve also as the motto of the unfortunate intellectual who must make his living by practicing a trade because he cannot find employment more suitable for his true talent and education.

consule Planco
KAWN-suu-leh PLAHN-koh
in the good old days

The literal translation of this phrase is "in the consulship of Plancus." Two consuls held office in Rome at any time. Their term of office under the republic was one year, but under the empire the term was reduced to a few months. Romans often referred to past years by the names of the consuls who then held office. Thus, Horace in his *Odes* referred to the carefree days of his youth as *consule Planco*. Plancus was consul in 42 B.C., when Horace was twenty-three and serving on the wrong side —under Brutus—at Philippi, where Augustus and Antony defeated Brutus and Cassius. Horace returned to Italy after the defeat to find that his family's property had been confiscated, his own prospects diminished. The phrase *consule Planco* has survived in the sense of "in the good old days." Since, justifiably or not, most people look back upon their early years as good times, Horace has given us a handy alternative for lectures to

our juniors that begin too often with "When I was young.
. . ." Nonetheless, recalling the experience of Plancus, we must
recognize the irony in *consule Planco*. The good old days too
often are good only in retrospect.

consummatum est
kawn-suum-MAH-tuum est
it is completed

Christ's last words on the cross, John 19:30

contra bonos mores
KAWN-trah BAW-nohs MOH-rays
against the best interests of society

This phrase, literally "contrary to good morals," is used in law
to describe an action or a contract considered harmful to the
moral welfare of society. Thus, a contract to commit a crime, for
example, is a contract *contra bonos mores* and therefore legally
void. Lawyers pronounce the phrase KAHN-trə BOH-nohs
MOH-reez. (See PRO BONO PUBLICO, a happier legal phrase.)

contraria contrariis curantur
kawn-TRAH-ree-ah kawn-TRAH-ree-ees
koo-RAHN-tuur
opposites are cured by opposites

The principle of allopathic medicine, the traditional form of
medicine, which seeks to fight disease by using remedies—an-
tibiotics are a good example—that produce effects totally different from the effects produced by the disease under treatment.
This principle is the direct opposite of that of homeopathic
medicine. (See SIMILIA SIMILIBUS CURANTUR.)

coram iudice (or judice)
KOH-rahm YOO-dih-keh
before a judge who has jurisdiction

This phrase, literally "in the presence of a judge," is used by lawyers to describe a hearing before a court that has the authority to act in the case. Lawyers pronounce *coram judice* (their preferred spelling) KOH-ram JOO-di-see.

coram nobis
KOH-rahm NOH-bees
before us

The legal phrase *coram nobis* denotes a writ intended to correct an injury caused by a mistake of the court. The phrase originated in English law, thus explaining the royal plural *nobis*. Lawyers pronounce *coram nobis* KOH-ram NOH-bis.

coram non iudice (or judice)
KOH-rahm nohn YOO-dih-keh
before a judge who does not have jurisdiction

This phrase, literally "in the presence of one not a judge," is used by lawyers to describe a hearing before a court that lacks authority or competence to rule in the matter. (See CORAM IUDICE.)

coram populo
KOH-rahm PAW-puu-loh
in public

This phrase, literally "in the presence of the people," was used by Horace in his *Ars Poetica*, in suggesting that a dramatist, in deference to sensibilities of audiences, should not depict murder on stage.

cornu copiae
KAWR-noo KOH-pee-ī
horn of plenty

Cornu copiae is also written in Latin as **cornucopia** (kawr-noo-KOH-pee-ah). The legend of Amalthea, the nymph who nursed Zeus when he was an infant, has it that she fed the young god with goat's milk. (Another version of the story has it that Amalthea was a goat that suckled the young Zeus.) Zeus endowed the horn of the goat with the capability of producing whatever the owner of the horn desired. Since Amalthea was the possessor of this *cornu copiae*, she could get from it whatever she wanted. Even today, the cornucopia is the symbol of abundance.

corpus delicti
KAWR-puus day-LIK-tee
the terrible evidence that a crime has been committed

The *corpus delicti*, literally "the body of the crime," is the fact or set of facts needed to establish that a crime has been committed. In murder, for example, it is proof that a person has been murdered. When we hear this phrase in old Hollywood detective movies, the district attorney is usually the character who complains to the chief of police that there is no *corpus delicti*, pronouncing it KOR-pəs də-LIK-tī, of course, and therefore there can be no prosecution of the heavy we all suspect. The audience squirms at the familiar complaint, believing the D.A. means the police cannot find the body of the victim. The confusion is with the English word "corpse," but what is really meant is that the district attorney cannot prove that a crime has been committed, even though a hacked-up corpse might be a good beginning. If the crime in question is arson, to take another example, the *corpus delicti* may be proof of arson, not merely a burned-out building; if the crime is burglary, evidence that a safe has been rifled, rather than merely an empty safe.

corpus iuris (or juris)
KAWR-puus YOO-ris
body of law

The collected laws of a nation, state, or city are its *corpus iuris*. Church law is **corpus iuris canonici** (kah-NOH-nih-kee), and civil law is **corpus iuris civilis** (KEE-wee-lis).

corrigenda
kawr-rih-GEN-dah
items to be corrected

The singular form, **corrigendum**, literally "that which is to be corrected," is ample evidence of the frailty of human beings: Because it is a singular form, it is almost never used. By contrast, the plural, *corrigenda*, is frequently found in manuscripts as well as in published books and journals. *Corrigenda* in its modern meaning calls attention to corrections that must be made here and there throughout a work before it is published (or republished).

Cras amet qui nunquam amavit;
Quique amavit, cras amet.
krahs AH-met kwee NUUN-kwahm ah-MAH-wit
KWEE-kweh ah-MAH-wit, krahs AH-met
May he love tomorrow who never has loved before;
And may he who has loved, love tomorrow as well.

This couplet forms the refrain of the *Pervigilium Veneris* (per-wih-GIH-lee-uum WEH-neh-ris), "The Night Watch of Love," written by an anonymous poet who obviously believed in love: yesterday, today, and tomorrow, as well as every day before and after. Samuel Butler, in *The Way of All Flesh*, expressed the same confidence in the desirability of love: " 'Tis better to have loved and lost than never to have loved at all."

credo quia absurdum est
KRAY-doh KWEE-ah ahb-SUUR-duum est
I believe it because it is unreasonable

A justification of faith on the basis that there is no need to understand: It is the essence of faith not to seek a rational explanation in matters spiritual. This profound statement of belief is also given as **credo quia impossibile** (im-paw-SIH-bih-leh) **est**, "I believe it because it is impossible."

crescite et multiplicamini
KREH-skih-teh et muul-tih-plih-KAH-mih-nee
increase and multiply

Motto of Maryland.

crescit eundo
KRAY-skit ay-UUN-doh
it grows as it goes

Motto of New Mexico.

cui bono?
KOO-ee BOH-noh
who stands to gain?

This expression, attributed by Cicero to a Roman judge and literally meaning "to whom for a benefit?" is mistakenly taken to mean "what good will it do?" Rather, it must be understood to be the question raised by anyone wise in the ways of the world: A new bridge is proposed for which there is no apparent need. Which contractor wants to make a fat profit from the project? A new weapon program is said to be essential to our national defense. Whose turn is it now in the military-industrial cost-overrun labyrinth? Both questions may be replaced by *cui bono?*

cuius regio eius religio
KOO-yuus RAY-gee-oh EH-yuus reh-LIH-gee-oh
the ruler of a territory chooses its religion

Historically, the religion practiced by the ruler of a region determined the religion practiced by his or her subjects. Today, *cuius regio eius religio*, literally "whose the region, his the religion," may be used in a broader sense. For example, the white shirt, striped tie, and vested dark suit dictated for male employees of certain corporations; the spectacle of football players, under compulsion, bowing their heads in prayer before a game (and then being told to "get out there and hit them hard").

cum grano salis
kuum GRAH-noh SAH-lis
with a grain of salt

One of the most familiar Latin expressions. When one does not fully believe something or someone, *cum grano salis* implies a certain caution or reserve. Salt was a valuable commodity in the ancient world, so a grain of salt is not be taken as a trivial matter. It is worth noting that the English word "salary" derives ultimately from the Latin: **Salarium** (sah-LAH-ree-uum) was the money allotted to Roman soldiers for purchase of salt, hence, their pay.

cum laude
kuum LOW-deh
with praise

A university degree awarded *cum laude* is the third rank of honors, **magna** (MAHG-nah) **cum laude**, "with great praise," is second in rank, while **summa** (SUUM-mah) **cum laude**, "with greatest praise," is the top rank. A student who has staggered through to a degree with barely passing grades is said jocularly to be graduated **summa cum difficultate** (dih-fih-kuul-TAH-teh), "with greatest difficulty."

cum privilegio
kuum pree-wih-LAY-gee-oh
with privilege

An authorized or licensed edition of a book is an edition *cum privilegio* or an **editio** (eh-DIH-tee-oh, "edition") **cum privilegio**.

cum tacent clamant
kuum TAH-kent KLAH-mahnt
silence is an admission of guilt

This expression, literally "when they remain silent they cry out," is from the first of Cicero's orations against Catiline, one of Cicero's political opponents. Despite the tradition of Western justice that a person accused of crime is not required to give evidence against himself, the popular view is that silence is an admission of guilt. Thus, *cum tacent clamant* is a powerful argument outside a court of law (and sometimes inside a jury room).

curae leves loquuntur ingentes stupent
KOO-rī LEH-ways loh-KWUUN-tuur in-GEN-tays
STUU-pent
minor losses can be talked away, profound ones strike us dumb

This maxim of Seneca's, from his play *Phaedra*, is more literally translated as "slight griefs talk, great ones are speechless." Seneca's observation may be tested at a wake, when conversation of the most inane sort occupies many of the people present, yet others speak not at all.

currente calamo
kuu-REN-teh KAH-lah-moh
with pen running on

Anything written without care or forethought can be described as having been written *currente calamo*: A writer who never stops to reflect need not take his pen from the page.

curriculum vitae
kuu-RIH-kuu-luum WEE-tī
a résumé

An academic who is asked to submit a written account of his qualifications usually compiles his *curriculum vitae*, literally "the course of (one's) life." Using the Latin expression instead of the mundane, albeit once-glamorous, word *résumé*, a French adoption, avoids association with the world of commerce. Because *curriculum vitae* is a mouthful, it is often referred to as a **c.v.** or as a **vita**, and the latter is pronounced VĪT-ə (in Latin WEE-tah).

custos morum
ḲUUS-tohs MOH-ruum
a censor

Custos means "guardian" or "watchman." Thus, a **custos incorruptissimus** (in-kaw-ruup-TIHS-sih-muus) is "a young man's guardian," since such a person can be trusted never to stray in any way; he is superlatively incorruptible. **Mores** (MOH-rays) means "morals," so *custos morum* is "the guardian of morals" and a Latin term for "censor."

dabit deus his quoque finem
DAH-bit DAY-uus hees KWAH-kweh FEE-nem
God will grant an end even to these (troubles)

This saying from Virgil's *Aeneid* counsels hope, even in the darkest hour. (For a similarly optimistic observation from Virgil, see FORSAN ET HAEC OLIM MEMINISSE IUVABIT.)

dabit qui dedit
DAH-bit kwee DEH-dit
he who has given will give

A suitable maxim for the professional fund-raiser: Those who once have contributed to a worthwhile cause can be counted upon to reach down deep again. It is for this reason that those of us who give even once to charity—or who buy once by mail order—soon find ourselves inundated with requests that we do so once again and again and again.

damnant quod non intelligunt
DAHM-nahnt kwawd nohn in-TEHL-lih-guunt
they condemn what they do not understand

The perennial cry of the obscure poet or struggling avant-gardist.

damnum absque iniuria (or injuria)
DAHM-nuum AHBS-kweh ihn-YOO-ree-ah
sorry, no basis for a lawsuit

This legal term, literally "loss without harm," refers to loss of property or violation of a right without possibility of legal redress. Not exactly the sort of thing on which attorneys thrive.

de asini umbra disceptare
day AH-sih-nee UUM-brah dih-skeh-PTAH-reh
"little things affect little minds"

This Latin phrase, freely rendered above in a line quoted from Disraeli's novel *Sybil*, may be translated literally as "to argue about the shadow of an ass." The phrase finds ready use in derogating the work of a lesser scholar who spends a lifetime explicating the unimportant, as well as in hushing the disputatious bore ever ready to quibble over the trivial.

de bono et malo
day BAW-noh et MAH-loh
come what may

The literal translation of this phrase is "of good and bad." When one has decided to forge ahead come what may, for better or for worse, the decision is made *de bono et malo*.

deceptio visus
day-KEH-ptee-oh WEE-soos
an optical illusion

Literally "a deception of vision."

de die in diem
day DEE-ay in DEE-em
continuously

Literally "from day to day," and also given as **diem ex die** (DEE-em eks DEE-ay), with the same meaning. "Those of us who are happily employed work *de die in diem*, never looking up from our work until we finish the task in hand." An apt rendering of either of the Latin phrases would be "day in, day out."

de duobus malis, minus est semper eligendum
deh doo-OH-buus MAH-lees MIH-nuus est SEM-pehr eh-lih-GEN-duum
choose the lesser of two evils

Recognizing the realities facing those who must often choose between less than perfect alternatives, Thomas à Kempis, the fifteenth-century theologian, adjures us in this Latin phrase to make the best of a bad situation, saying literally, "of two evils, the lesser is always to be chosen."

de facto
day FAH-ktoh
in reality

This common expression, pronounced di FAK-toh in English, is literally translated as "from the fact." It differentiates that which exists in fact (*de facto*) from that which exists legally (*de iure* or *de jure*, day YOO-reh). Thus, *de facto* rulers, in contrast with *de iure* rulers, are calling the signals even though no legal process has been employed in establishing their power. Again, *de facto* segregation may reflect custom or practice, rather than the law of the land, yet segregation it is.

de gustibus non est disputandum
day GUU-stih-buus nohn est dih-spuu-TAHN-duum
there's no accounting for tastes

This widely used expression, literally "about tastes there is no disputing," wisely tells us that taste is a personal matter. Since no amount of persuasion can succeed in changing a person's taste—and rightfully so—it is better not to argue about matters of personal preference. In time, a person's taste may change, but not because of anything others may say. This saying is sometimes given as **de gustibus et coloribus** (et kaw-LOH-rih-buus, "and colors") **non disputandum**, more often merely as *de gustibus*, "concerning tastes."

Dei gratia
DAY-ee GRAH-tee-ah
by the grace of God

Found in such expressions as **Regina** (ray-GEE-nah) **Dei Gratia**, "Queen by the Grace of God," and **Imperator** (im-peh-RAH-tawr) **Dei Gratia**, "Emperor by the Grace of God." The implication is that anyone functioning *Dei gratia* has direct access to the Divinity.

de integro
day IN-teh-groh

anew

Anything that commences with the past obliterated from memory begins *de integro*. (See DE NOVO.)

de iure (or de jure)
day YOO-reh

sanctioned by law

See DE FACTO.

delenda est Carthago
day-LEN-dah est kahr-TAH-goh

Carthage must be destroyed

The story behind this phrase is well worth recounting. For two centuries or so, Carthage was the only real rival to Rome in the western Mediterranean. In fact, until the two superpowers came into conflict in Sicily in 264 B.C.—war broke out because Rome feared Carthaginian expansionism in southern Italy —Carthage had been the dominant power. Rome prevailed in the First Punic War (264–261), but the peace terms left Carthage still strong enough to threaten Rome. Sure enough, there was a Second Punic War (218–201). This time, Hannibal's brilliant strategy nearly destroyed Rome, but Scipio Africanus, the Roman general, defeated Hannibal—perhaps at Zama, an ancient town in present-day Tunisia—in the decisive battle of that war, and Carthage was no longer a power to reckon with. Half a century later, when Carthage still was not a threat to Rome, war broke out once again, in part because of the influence of Cato the Elder, who repeatedly egged the Roman Senate on with his ominous phrase *delenda est Carthago*: "Carthage must be destroyed." Since Carthage was not a match for Rome's military power, the outcome of this Third Punic War (149–146) was predictable: Soon enough the Carthaginians, led to believe they would be given generous peace terms, were tricked into surrendering. But once peace prevailed, the great city of Carthage was destroyed by the Romans, and a century was to pass before Carthage was resettled and became a prosperous city once more. Cato's *delenda est Carthago* survives as an ironic reminder that a ruling clique in a powerful nation can have its way in crushing a helpless rival if it musters the rhetoric to stir irrational passions.

delineavit
day-lee-nay-AH-wit
he (or she) drew (this)

An indication, along with the artist's name, of the creator of a painting, drawing, or sculpture: *delineavit Publius* or *del. Publius*, "drawn by Publius."

delirium tremens
day-LEE-ree-uum TREH-mens
the d.t.'s

Literally "trembling delirium," *delirium tremens* is the mental disorder associated with overindulgence in drinking. The afflicted person characteristically trembles excessively and hallucinates. *Delirium tremens* is commonly given the English pronunciation də-LIR-ee-əm TREE-mənz.

de minimis non curat praetor
day MIH-nih-mees nohn KOO-raht PRĪ-tawr
don't bother me with petty matters

The literal translation of this expression is "a praetor does not occupy himself with petty matters." A praetor—the English word is pronounced PREET-ər—in ancient Rome was a magis-

trate who assisted the consuls by administering justice and commanding armies. In Caesar's time, there were sixteen **praetores**
(prī-TOH-rays). Since a praetor was a busy man, we can appreciate his insistence on saving his time for important matters.
Today, anyone wanting to suggest that he or she is above small
matters may use this phrase, inevitably with the intention of
impressing others with the importance of the concerns that
normally occupy an important person's time. A related expression is the legal precept **de minimis non curat lex** (leks), "the law
does not concern itself with trifles," which is used to justify
refusal by a court, particularly an appellate court, to hear a suit,
on the basis that a court's time must not be taken up with
matters of small import. This phrase, often abbreviated *de minimis*, explains why income tax payments that are a few dollars
short of what they should be are sometimes accepted without
complaint.

de mortuis nihil nisi bonum
day MAWR-too-ees NIH-hil NIH-sih BAW-nuum
speak kindly of the dead

Tradition has it that Chilon of Sparta, one of the wise men of
sixth-century B.C. Greece, is the author of this saying, literally
"of the dead, (say) nothing but good." (Of course, Chilon used
Greek rather than Latin, so what we have here is the Latin
translation.) The advice to all of us that one should speak well
of the recently dead or remain silent is at least as old as Homer.
Nihil, "nothing," is also given as a contraction, **nil** (neel).

de nihilo nihil
day NIH-hih-loh NIH-hil
nothing comes from nothing

Persius, the first-century A.D. Roman poet, advises us in his
Satires that effort is required to produce anything of value.
He goes on to tell us that anything once produced cannot be-
come nothing again: **in nihilum nil posse reverti** (in NIH-

hih-luum neel PAW-seh reh-WEHR-tee). Persius is believed to
have been parodying Lucretius (first century B.C.), who pro-
pounded the physical theories of Epicurus (fourth century
B.C.). As a cynical comment, *de nihilo nihil* can be distorted
to denigrate a failed work as the product of a person of little
talent. The implication is, "How can we expect better from
such a source?"

de novo
day NAW-woh
anew

Like DE INTEGRO, *de novo* is an expression used in describing
a fresh start. "Let's forget the past and begin *de novo*."

Deo favente
DAY-oh fah-WEN-teh
with God's favor

An expression used to invoke God's cooperation in ensuring
success for an action about to begin or to express gratitude for
the success of an activity completed successfully. "*Deo favente*,
I will pass my examination." "I have always been able to make
a good living, *Deo favente*."

Deo gratias
DAY-oh GRAH-tee-ahs
thanks to God

When an enterprise has turned out well, one may say *Deo
gratias* or DEO FAVENTE. *Deo gratias* appears frequently in
Latin prayers, but it is also used jocularly. "As the curtain came
down on the opera after five long hours, some were shouting
bravo while others were muttering *Deo gratias*."

Deo iuvante (or Deo juvante)
DAY-oh yoo-WAHN-teh
with God's help

This expression, also given as **Deo adiuvante** or **Deo adjuvante** (ahd-yoo-WAHN-teh), has the same intent and is used in the same manner as DEO FAVENTE.

de omni re scibili et quibusdam aliis
day AWM-nee ray SKIH-bih-lee et KWIH-buus-dahm
AH-lee-ees
I know everything worth knowing, and more

De omni re scibili, literally "of all the things one can know," was the pretentious title of a work by a fifteenth-century Italian scholar, Pico della Mirandola, who prided himself on being able to debate with anyone on any subject. In derision, someone (perhaps Voltaire) added to it *et quibusdam aliis*, literally "and even of several other things." The result is an elegant phrase one can use to puncture the pomposity of a self-proclaimed expert on everything under the sun.

Deo optimo maximo
DAY-oh AW-ptih-moh MAH-ksih-moh
to God, the best, the greatest

Once a favorite dedication (abbreviated **D.O.M.**) for a work of art. (See DOMINO OPTIMO MAXIMO.)

Deo volente
DAY-oh waw-LEN-teh
God willing

Yet another expression (abbreviated **D.V.**) used to enlist the aid of the deity when initiating an enterprise or looking forward to the future. "*Deo volente*, we will all be here next year to celebrate our fifty-first anniversary."

de pilo pendet
day PIH-loh PEN-det
we've reached the critical stage

This expression, literally "it hangs by a hair," is used to describe the tense moment when a sickness, a sports event, a military action, or the like appears to be in the lap of the gods. *De pilo pendet* derives from the situation in which Damocles found himself: Dionysius I, the tyrant of Syracuse, in order to demonstrate that the life of a ruler was no bed of roses, had Damocles, a fawning member of the court, seated at a royal banquet with a sword suspended over his head by a single hair. We recall Damocles in the phrase "sword of Damocles," with the meaning "an impending disaster," and our word "impending" has its origin in **pendere** (PEN-deh-reh), the Latin word for "hang."

de profundis
day praw-FUUN-dees
out of the depths (of despair)

A cry of deepest anguish, from the opening words of Psalm 130: "Out of the depths have I cried unto thee, O Lord." This psalm is often read in the Catholic burial service, but *de profundis* has other associations: Oscar Wilde, after being imprisoned in 1895 for homosexual practices, wrote an essay called "De Profundis," which was published posthumously.

de proprio motu
day PRAW-pree-oh MOH-too
spontaneously

Literally "of one's (or its) own motion." "Everything happened *de proprio motu* from then on; we played no further part in shaping events."

De Rerum Natura
day REH-ruum nah-TOO-rah
On the Nature of Things

A philosophic poem by Lucretius, first century B.C., outlining a science of the universe based on the philosophies of Democritus and Epicurus, and attempting to prove that all things in nature operate without reliance on the supernatural.

desipere in loco
day-SIH-peh-reh in LAW-koh
to play the fool on occasion

Horace, in his *Odes*, wrote **dulce est** (DUUL-keh est) **desipere in loco**, literally "sweet it is (*dulce est*) to relax at the proper time." Students who complete their examinations successfully and writers who finish a book on schedule, for example, know how to shuck off their dignity and enjoy themselves fully, knowing their work is done. The rest of us, who spend our time in idleness when faced with pressing obligations, never know the restorative value of that great delight, earned leisure.

deus ex machina
DAY-uus eks MAH-kih-nah
an unlikely and providential intervention

Deus ex machina, literally "a god out of a machine," describes an unexpected occurrence that rescues someone or something from an apparently hopeless predicament: An impoverished widow about to be evicted receives a legacy from a long-lost aunt or wins first prize in a million-dollar lottery. This is the stuff that bad fiction or drama is made of, so it is no surprise that *deus ex machina* is usually applied to narrative works, especially to the work of playwrights and novelists who find themselves enmeshed in complexities of their own devising and incapable of bringing their plots to a close without relying on improbable coincidence. Thus, when the U.S. Cavalry—in vintage Hollywood style—comes over the hill just as the long-lost brother of its commanding officer is about to be scalped, the writer has resorted to *deus ex machina*. The expression has its origin in ancient Greek theater, especially in certain plays of Euripides. When the complexities of plot and character appeared incapable of resolution, a god was set down on stage by a mechanical crane to sort out things and make them right. Greek gods could do anything.

Deus Misereatur

DAY-uus mih-seh-ray-AH-tuur

May God Have Mercy

The title of Psalm 67, which begins *Deus misereatur* and continues (in English) "and bless us, and cause His countenance to shine upon us."

Deus vobiscum

DAY-uus woh-BEES-kuum

God be with you

An appropriate saying, literally "God with you," to use when taking one's leave. The singular form is **Deus tecum** (TAY-kuum).

Deus vult

DAY-uus wuult

God wills it

Battle cry of the First Crusade, in the final years of the eleventh century, which resulted in recovery of the Holy Land from the Muslims: The people who had gathered to hear an address by Pope Urban II at the Council of Clermont in 1095 responded *Deus vult*. Since most armies normally proceed on the basis that God favors them or orders them to fight, it is not surprising that the Crusaders used *Deus vult* as a battle cry. The motto of the German armies during the two great wars of the twentieth century was *Gott Mitt Uns*, "God (is) with us."

diem ex die
DEE-em eks DEE-ay
continuously

See DE DIE IN DIEM.

diem perdidi
DEE-em PEHR-dih-dee
another day wasted

Titus, emperor of Rome, having passed an entire day without performing a good deed, is reported to have said, *Diem perdidi*, literally "I have lost a day." Anyone who has a job to do that requires sustained effort in order to meet a tight deadline may use the phrase to express despair at the end of an unproductive day, another day down the tube.

dies faustus
DEE-ays FOW-stuus
an auspicious day

The Romans paid a great deal of attention to omens. For example, a Roman who saw a meteor or a flight of birds would look upon the display as an indication of a *dies faustus*, literally "a day bringing good fortune." (*Faustus* is the perfect passive participle of **faveo** (FAH-weh-oh), "favor.") **Dies infaustus** (in-FOW-stuus) has the opposite meaning.

Dies Irae
DEE-ays EE-rī
Day of Wrath

A thirteenth-century Latin hymn on the Day of Judgment, sung at the requiem mass.

dii penates
DEE-ee peh-NAH-tays
guardians of the household

Dii penates were the household gods of the ancient Romans, a people given to a plethora of gods. *Dii*, the plural of **deus** (DAY-uus), "god," is also written **dei** (DAY-ee) and **di** (dee). *Penates* alone also means "household gods." However expressed, the intention is clear: Roman families and their homes were looked after by special deities. (See LARES ET PENATES.)

dirigo
DEE-rih-goh
I direct

Motto of Maine, there pronounced də-REE-goh, and also translated as "I guide" or "I lead the way." The implication is that God directs, despite the popular wisdom that New Englanders—witness "As Maine goes, so goes the nation"—take direction from no one but themselves.

dis aliter visum
dees AH-lih-tehr WEE-suum
man proposes, God disposes

A literal translation for Virgil's *dis aliter visum*, in the *Aeneid*, is "it seemed otherwise to the gods." An appropriate expression for rationalizing a failed effort.

disiecta (or disjecta) membra
dih-SYEH-ktah MEM-brah
fragments

A phrase, literally "scattered limbs," used to describe brief quotations from literary works. Horace wrote of **disiecti** (dih-SYEH-ktee) **membra poetae** (poh-AY-tī), "limbs of a dismembered poet," suggesting that one can perceive the quality of good poets even in brief quotations from their works.

disputandi pruritus ecclesiarum scabies
dih-spuu-TAHN-dee proo-REE-tuus
ek-KLAY-see-AH-ruum SKAH-bee-ays
the theologian's urge to debate is an incurable disease

Sir Henry Wotton, 1568–1639, an English poet and diplomat, wrote this sentence, literally "an itch for disputation is the mange of the churches," in *A Panegyric to King Charles*, and it was later used as part of Wotton's own tombstone inscription. (Wotton is also recalled for his definition of an ambassador: "an honest man sent to lie abroad for the good of his country.")

ditat Deus
DEE-taht DAY-uus
God enriches

Motto of Arizona.

divide et impera
DEE-wih-deh et IHM-peh-rah
divide and rule

This ancient political maxim, adopted by Machiavelli, is also given as **divide ut regnes** (uut REH-gnays) and as **divide ut imperes** (IHM-peh-rays), all of which mean "divide in order to

rule." One stratagem of a wily leader is to encourage his followers to squabble continually among themselves, making it easy
for him to have his own way.

divina natura dedit agros, ars humana aedificavit urbes
dih-WEE-nah nah-TOO-rah DEH-dit AH-grohs ahrs
hoo-MAH-nah ī-dih-fih-KAH-wit UUR-bays
God made the country, and man made the town

A maxim, literally "godlike nature gave us the fields, human
skill built the cities," of Marcus Terentius Varro, first-century
B.C. Roman scholar, in *De Re Rustica*.

Divinitatis Doctor
dee-wee-nih-TAH-tis DAWK-tawr
Doctor of Divinity

Abbreviated **D.D.** It is worth mentioning that the Latin word
doctor means "teacher," not "physician."

dixi
DEE-ksee
that settles the matter

This word, literally "I have spoken," signals that "I will say no
more on the matter, and no one else may speak further."

docendo discimus
daw-KEN-doh DIH-skih-muus
we learn by teaching

A maxim well understood by inspired teachers and leading to
the advice **doce ut discas** (DAW-kay uut DIH-skahs), "teach in
order to learn."

doctus cum libro
DAW-ktuus kuum LIH-broh
having book learning

This expression, literally "learned with a book," describes those of us who lack practical knowledge.

Domine, dirige nos
DAW-mih-neh DEE-rih-geh nohs
Lord, direct us

Motto of London.

Domino optimo maximo
DAW-mih-noh AW-ptih-moh MAH-ksih-moh
to the Lord God, supreme ruler of the world

This phrase, literally "to the Lord, best and greatest," is the motto of the Benedictine Order. It is included here for the edification of those who are fond of an after-dinner glass of Benedictine and brandy. On the label of a bottle of Benedictine, a liqueur originally made by monks of the Benedictine Order, appears **D.O.M.**, the abbreviation of *Domino optimo maximo*. (See DEO OPTIMO MAXIMO.)

Dominus illuminatio mea
DAW-mih-nuus ih-LOO-mih-NAH-tee-oh MAY-ah
the Lord is my light

Motto of Oxford University.

Dominus vobiscum
DAW-mih-nuus woh-BEES-kuum
God be with you

Another way to bid farewell. The singular form is **Dominus tecum** (TAY-kuum). (See DEUS VOBISCUM.)

donec eris felix, multos numerabis amicos
DAW-nek EH-ris FAY-liks MUUL-tohs
nuu-meh-RAH-bis ah-MEE-kohs
when you're successful, everyone wants to be your friend

This observation, literally "as long as you are fortunate, you will have many friends," from Ovid's *Tristia* reflects bitterly on human nature. It concludes with **tempora si fuerint nubila, solus eris** (TEM-paw-rah see FOO-eh-rint NOO-bih-lah SOH-luus EH-ris), literally "if clouds appear, you will be alone." Even in ancient Rome, there were fair-weather friends.

dramatis personae
DRAH-mah-tis per-SOH-nī
cast of characters

This familiar expression, literally "the persons of the drama," although primarily denoting the characters or actors in a play, can be taken also as the characters in a novel, poem, film, etc., as well as the participants in the events of everyday life. "The hostages and their captors constituted a familiar *dramatis personae*."

ducit amor patriae
DOO-kit AH-mawr PAH-tree-ī
love of country guides me

The motto of the patriot, literally "love of country guides." (See DULCE ET DECORUM . . .)

dulce est desipere in loco
DUUL-keh est day-SIH-peh-reh in LAW-koh
sweet it is to relax at the proper time

  See DESIPERE IN LOCO.

dulce et decorum est pro patria mori
DUUL-keh et deh-KOH-ruum est proh PAH-tree-ah
MAW-ree
there's no greater honor than to die for one's country

  We meet these words in Horace's *Odes*, literally "it is sweet
and fitting to die for the fatherland."

dum spiro spero
duum SPEE-roh SPEH-roh
while I breathe, I hope

  A motto of South Carolina. (See ANIMIS OPIBUSQUE PARATI.)

dum tacent clamant
duum TAH-kent KLAH-mahnt
their silence speaks volumes

  The literal meaning of this saying is "though they are silent
they cry aloud." Silence may have great significance, in certain
situations even constituting an admission of guilt.

dum vita est spes est
duum WEE-tah est SPAYS est
while there's life, there's hope

dum vivimus vivamus
duum WEE-wih-muus wee-WAH-muus
while we live, let us live

The motto of the Epicureans, followers of Epicurus, who taught that pleasure is the goal of morality, but defined a life of pleasure as one of honor, prudence, and justice—in short, advocating living one's life to make for tranquility of body and mind. These teachings were corrupted later—epicureanism today is equated with self-indulgence and luxurious tastes.

dura lex sed lex
DOO-rah leks sed leks
the law is hard, but it is the law

Just about the only thing one can say when trying to convince others to pay their income tax or to obey a law generally considered unfair or harsh.

dux femina facti
duuks FAY-mih-nah FAH-ktee
cherchez la femme

We have Virgil, in the *Aeneid*, to thank for this Latin phrase, literally "a woman was the leader in the deed." We must also bow in the direction of countless fictional detectives for their adoption of Dumas's advice, *cherchez la femme* if you want to get to the bottom of things.

ecce homo
EK-keh HAW-moh
behold the man

The Latin translation of the words Pontius Pilate (John 19) used in showing the people the bound Christ wearing the crown of thorns. *Ecce homo* is the title taken for many paintings depicting Christ in this condition.

ecce signum
EK-keh SIH-gnuum
look at the proof

This phrase, literally "behold the sign," adjures us to examine the evidence, the proof. In *Henry IV*, *Part I*, Falstaff boasts of his encounter with a small army of attackers bent on his destruction: "I am eight times thrust through the doublet, four through the hose; my buckler cut through and through; my sword hacked like a handsaw—*ecce signum!*"

e contrario
ay kawn-TRAH-ree-oh
on the contrary

editio cum notis variorum
ay-DIH-tee-oh kuum NOH-tees wah-ree-OH-ruum
an edition with the notes of various persons

An edition of a literary text, called in English a "variorum (va-ree-OHR-əm) edition," that offers variant readings of the text as well as notes and commentary by scholars. (See VARI-ORUM.)

editio princeps
ay-DIH-tee-oh PRIN-keps
first edition

Of ancient texts, the first printed edition.

editio vulgata
ay-DIH-tee-oh wuul-GAH-tah
common edition

See TERRA ES, TERRAM IBIS.

e.g.
for example

See EXEMPLI GRATIA.

eheu fugaces labuntur anni
eh-HEHOO fuu-GAH-kays lah-BUUN-tuur AHN-nee
alas, the fleeting years glide by

A sad line from Horace's *Odes*, reminding us—as though we need help in remembering—that Maxwell Anderson was on the money when he told us that our "days dwindle down to a precious few." *Eheu*, alas! (Turn quickly to CARPE DIEM.)

eiusdem (or ejusdem) farinae
ay-YUUS-dem fah-REE-nī
birds of a feather

This expression, literally "of the same flour," is used to characterize people of the same nature—"cut from the same cloth"—usually in a pejorative sense.

e libris
ay LIH-brees

See EX LIBRIS.

emeritus
ay-MEH-rih-tuus
having served his time

This word has its origins in Roman military tradition, with the meaning of "a soldier who has served his time honorably." In modern usage, it is applied to a university officer who is rewarded for faithful service with the rank, for example, of "emeritus professor." The designation, pronounced ə-MER-ə-təs in English, carries no formal obligation to the institution, but usually entitles the person so designated to continue to use the facilities of the institution and to attend ceremonies as an honored member of the academic community. Emeritus rank is the academic equivalent of the gold watch given to good old what's-his-name upon retirement. University women who retire from academic life may be given **emerita** (ay-MEH-rih-tah; in English, ə-MER-ə-tə) rank, although some institutions eschew this feminine form.

ense et aratro
EN-seh et ah-RAH-troh
serving in war and in peace

The motto, literally "with sword and plow," of the farmer who serves his country by putting down the plow, **aratrum** (ah-RAH-truum), in time of war to take up the sword, **ensis** (EN-sees), for his country. In time of peace, he returns to his farm to serve his country once again. The motto applies equally well to any civilians who leave their peacetime jobs to take up arms for their country. Isaiah looks forward to the time when "They shall beat their swords into plowshares, and their spears into pruning hooks; nation shall not lift up sword against nation, neither shall they learn war any more."

ense petit placidam sub libertate quietem
EN-seh PEH-tit PLAH-kih-dahm suub
lee-behr-TAH-teh kwee-AY-tem
by the sword she seeks peaceful quiet under liberty

Motto of Massachusetts, making the case for military preparedness for the sake of ensuring peace.

e pluribus unum
ay PLOO-rih-buus OO-nuum
one out of many

Motto of the United States of America, indicating that a single nation was made by uniting many states.

ergo
EHR-goh
therefore

errare humanum est
ehr-RAH-reh hoo-MAH-nuum est
to err is human

The recognition, also given as **errare est humanum**, that erasers are attached to pencils for good reason. Alexander Pope, in "An Essay on Criticism": "To err is human, to forgive, divine."

erratum
ehr-RAH-tuum
error

An error in printing or writing is given the dignified appellation *erratum*, plural **errata** (ehr-RAH-tah). An *errata* (English pronunciation e-RAHT-ə) is a list of such errors.

esse quam videri
ES-seh kwahm wih-DAY-ree
to be rather than seem

Motto of North Carolina.

est modus in rebus
est MAW-duus in RAY-buus
choose the middle ground

With these words from Horace's *Satires*, literally "there is a proper measure in things," we are advised against extremes.

esto perpetua
EH-stoh per-PEH-too-ah
may she live forever

Motto of Idaho. Said to be the dying words of Fra Paolo Sarpi (1552–1623), historian and philosopher, speaking of his native Venice.

et al.
abbreviation of **et alii, et aliae, et alia**

This abbreviation is used in writing to avoid a lengthy listing. **Et alii** (et AH-lee-ee) is masculine, so it is properly used in speech to mean "and other men" when preceded by the name of a male or to mean "and other people." **Et aliae** (AH-lee-ī) is feminine, so it is properly used in speech to mean "and other women." **Et alia** (AH-lee-ah) is neuter, so it is properly used in speech to mean "and other things." Educated persons do not pronounce the abbreviation *et al.* "And others" is said for *et al*.

et cetera
et KAY-teh-rah
and so on

This familiar phrase, pronounced et SET-ər-ə in English and used only when speaking of things, not people, literally means "and the rest." In speech, its abbreviation, etc., is given the pronunciation of the full phrase.

et hoc genus omne
et hawk GEH-nuus AWM-neh
and all that sort

This expression, literally "and everything of the kind," is used to indicate others of a class of persons or things. It finds use as a pretentious substitute for *et cetera*.

etiam atque etiam
EH-tee-ahm AHT-kweh EH-tee-ahm
again and again

et nunc et semper
et nuunk et SEM-pehr
from now on

Literally "now and forever."

et sic de similibus
et seek day sih-MIH-lih-buus
and that goes for the others too

This phrase, literally "and so of similar (people or things)," is used to suggest that whatever has been said of one person or topic under discussion holds true for related matters as well. (See AB UNO DISCE OMNES.)

et tu, Brute
et too BROO-teh
so you're mixed up in this too

According to tradition, reflected in Shakespeare's *Julius Caesar*, the final words of Caesar, falling before the conspirators' knives: "*Et tu Brute*! (literally "You also Brutus") Then fall Caesar." The line, memorized by all schoolchildren, reflects Plutarch's account of the death of Caesar. Caesar resisted his attackers until he realized that Brutus, his trusted ally, had joined in the attack. Blessed with this provenance, *et tu Brute* has become the classic recognition of betrayal by a trusted friend.

et ux.
and wife

The lawyer's abbreviation for **et uxor** (et UUK-sawr): "John Smith *et ux*." "And wife" is said for *et ux*.

ex aequo et bono
eks Ī-kwoh et BAW-noh
equitably

A principled person does everything *ex aequo et bono*, literally "according to what is just and good."

ex animo
eks AH-nih-moh
sincerely

A person who speaks from the bottom of his heart speaks *ex animo*, literally "from the heart."

ex cathedra
eks KAH-teh-drah
with authority

When a pope speaks *ex cathedra*, literally "from the chair," he is considered to speak infallibly, and the chair he speaks from is the papal throne. Thus, when experts speak authoritatively on matters in their fields of knowledge, we may say that they speak *ex cathedra* (in English, eks kə-THEE-drə) or that they have made *ex cathedra* statements. We may also apply *ex cathedra* ironically to dogmatic pronouncements by the pretentious self-proclaimed expert. It must be pointed out that before the *cathedra* was the pope's chair —indeed, before there were popes—it was the chair of a teacher.

excelsior
eks-KEHL-see-awr
ever upward

Literally "higher," *excelsior* is pronounced ek-SEL-see-ər in English and serves as the motto of the State of New York.

exceptio probat regulam
eks-KEH-ptee-oh PRAW-baht RAY-guu-lahm
the exception establishes the rule

This proverb, shortened from the legal maxim **exceptio probat regulam in casibus non exceptis** (in KAH-sih-buus nohn eks-KEH-ptees, "in the cases not excepted"), is mistakenly taken as "the exception proves the rule," leading the unwary to think that any self-respecting rule must have an exception. What is meant is that the existence of an exception to a rule provides an opportunity to test the validity of a rule: Finding an exception to a rule enables us to define the rule more precisely, confirming its applicability to those items truly covered by the rule.

excudit
eks-KOO-dit
made by

A printer or engraver's mark, literally "he (or she) struck (this)," used to identify the person who executed the work. The abbreviation for *excudit* is **excud.**

exeat
EKS-ay-aht
permission to be absent

An *exeat*, literally "let him (or her) go forth," is an official permission granted to a priest to leave a diocese or monastery. In British universities, an *exeat* is permission granted for temporary absence from a college.

exegi monumentum aere perennius
eks-AY-gee MAW-nuu-MEN-tuum AH-eh-reh
pehr-EHN-nee-uus
I have raised a monument more durable than bronze

Horace started his final ode with these words, suggesting that his *Odes* would bring him immortality. Only the likes of a Horace should apply this sentence to their own work.

exempli gratia
eks-EHM-plee GRAH-tee-ah
for instance

This expression, literally "for the sake of example," is always abbreviated **e.g.** in English. It is used correctly to introduce an example, incorrectly to mean "that is." (See ID EST.)

exeunt
EKS-ay-uunt
they leave the stage